This book is dedicated to all the children whom I have known and loved; and those with whom I have had the pleasure of working. Without them this could not have been possible. Their joy, enthusiasm and progress exemplify what it is all about. They provide evidence of the boundless potential of a child and give us reason to believe and carry on.

~

TABLE OF CONTENTS

LIST OF TABLES

CHAPTER ONE

Puff, puff, chug, chug, went the Little Blue Engine. "I think I can, I think I can, I think I can...."

- The Little Engine That Could
By Watty Piper

Introduction

Children's belief in their ability to perform has a greater impact on achievement than actual skills and talent. Perceived self-efficacy affects the types of tasks a child will attempt, the effort the child will exert and the responsibility the child will take for success or failure. Self-efficacy is defined as the belief in one's capabilities to exercise the course of action necessary to achieve particular goals or outcomes. Self-efficacy beliefs influence the way people think, feel, motivate themselves, and act (Bandura, 1997). Self-efficacy has been linked to the choices and actions that a child will take in the course of a lifetime (Bandura; Bouffard-Bouchard, 1990; Fasko & Fasko, 1998; Schunk & Swartz, 1993). The purpose of this book is to provide a self-efficacy intervention with children in an effort to prepare them to meet the challenges and setbacks that life brings and direct them toward the path of reaching their potential.

The studies listed above indicate that at the foundation of healthy development in children is the belief that their actions are effective and that they have the power to produce change. Schunk & Swartz (1993) state that task involvement and effort increase as the sense of efficacy is heightened. Those with low self-efficacy often will not attempt tasks that may be within their realm of capability. There is a difference between possessing skills and utilizing them effectively to achieve goals or accomplish a task (Bouffard-Bouchard, 1990). Self-efficacy is a personal judgment regarding whether one has the skills to achieve a particular outcome (Powers, Sowers & Stevens, 1995). These authors state, "Youth who exhibit high levels of self-efficacy believe that they have the capabilities to accomplish their goals and will achieve their goals if they exercise those capabilities." (p. 34).

The children participating in this research project were deemed at risk based on the data profiles of their neighborhoods. The neighborhoods were characterized by poverty, with a neighborhood average of 36% of the children living below poverty (New York City Administration for Children's Services 1998). This was well above the

1

national average of 18.9% of children across American living in poverty that year (Weinberg, 1999). A prudent search of the literature on risk and resilience cites poverty as a major risk factor for children (Benard, 1993; Brooks, 2006; Fall & McLeod, 2001; Garmezy, 1983; Howard & Dryden, 1999; Kim-Cohen, Moffit, Caspi & Taylor, 2004; Little, Axford & Morpeth, 2004; Rak & Patterson, 1996; Smokowski, 1998).

Risk, Resilience and Protective Factors

In seeking to find means of enhancing self-efficacy in children who may lack opportunities to acquire the necessary skills to face challenges, the author explored the literature on risk, resilience and protective factors. It has become increasingly evident that many children have the capacity to adapt and triumph over extreme adversity.

For practical purposes, the term "risk" has been used to justify research and intervention strategies. Traditionally, the notion of risk derived from a medical model and epidemiological studies, referring to an individual's susceptibility to disease. The term was "problem focused", had derogatory connotations, inferring that the problem lay within individuals and rendered them vulnerable to negative outcomes (Brendtro & Longhurst, 2005; Little et al., 2004; Smokowski, 1998). More recently the focus has shifted from the individual to the environment and social conditions such as poverty, racial discrimination, injustice, limited opportunities, child abuse and neglect, parental conflict, large family size, having criminal parents, and inadequate parenting (Brooks, 2006; Harvey & Delfabbro, 2004; Horn & Chen 1998; Kim-Cohen et al., 2004; Little et al., 2004; Smokowski). Risk, nevertheless, implies need. This stimulates researchers to explore risks and find ways to address them or help individuals meet the challenges they pose. This has resulted in seeking answers through protective factors that aid in fostering resilience and contribute to at-risk children's success through amelioration of the risk factors they may face.

Resilience emerged from psychopathology as a reaction, or adaptation to risk (Smokowski, 1998). The concept of resilience was the focus of longitudinal studies and provided valuable information concerning the developmental outcome of children (Garmezy, 1983; Howard & Dryden, 1999; Rak & Paterson, 1996; Rutter, 1987; Werner & Smith, 1992). Embracing the notion that all children deserve the opportunity to reach their full potential, these researchers looked at the outcome of children who have had to

2

overcome obstacles and disadvantages. They studied the scores of children growing up amidst poverty, violence and other hardships and discovered that many of them seem to fare well even in the face of adversity.

Other authors are in agreement that some children have the potential to overcome risks in their environment and succeed regardless of challenging circumstances (Brooks, 2006; Brown, 2004; Connell, Spencer & Aber, 1994; Harvey & Delfabbro, 2004; Horn & Chen, 1998; Kim-Cohen et al., 2004; Little et al., 2004; Smokowski, 1998). These authors recognize that risk is minimized through protective factors that enhance resilience. Brown states, "Adaptability is surely what distinguishes resilient children from vulnerable" (p. 75). Brown discusses the role of mentors or supportive adults in promoting resilience in children faced with obstacles. Brooks makes suggestions for strengthening resilience in children through the schools by providing caring adults and maximizing opportunities. Some of the resilience factors described are temperament of the child, effective parenting, intelligence, self-esteem, self-efficacy, supportive adults and opportunities. Brooks asserts that resilience develops through interaction with the environment; therefore, interventions can be developed to promote resilience.

Connell and colleagues (1994) conducted a study with poor African-American inner-city children in an effort to address educational problems, assessing indicators of "context, self and action" and their relationship to measures of risk and resilient outcomes in school (p. 494). The results suggest that the young participants in the study report that family support, a sense of control over their success and failure, feelings of self-worth and emotional security regulate their actions in school "over and above the influence of their family's and their neighborhood's economic conditions..." (p. 503). The process model guiding the study predicted both positive and negative outcomes and lends support to the understanding of the relationship between risk and resilience. The authors make suggestions for interventions that would enhance the youth's belief in their ability to produce desired outcomes and improve peer relationships.

Harvey and Delfabbro (2004) explored resilience with "disadvantaged youth". They define these young people as "disadvantaged" due to factors such as social economic status, ethnicity, and history of abuse and acknowledge that many of the risk factors described here will remain a problem for young people and pose threats to healthy

3

development. However, they recognize that people respond differently to disadvantage and risk; many children are able to overcome adversity. They cite several long-term research projects that affirm this and describe methods to enhance resilience in young people, such as teaching coping skills, supportive adults and providing reinforcement of behavior through rewards.

Horn and Chen (1998) conducted a study with at-risk students to determine whether factors that contributed to success in graduating from high school continued to be effective in making the transition to college. The findings showed that discussions with parents around school-related matters, having peers who went on to college, and participating in college preparatory activities and outreach all played a role in attending college. However, the parent and peer influences were more predictive than college preparation involvement. Some of the risk factors of the students, identified by Horn and Chen, were: lowest socioeconomic quartile, single-parent family, older sibling dropping out of high school, frequent change of schools, low grades and repeat of earlier grades. The results of this study confirm that intervention was instrumental in helping high-risk students go to college.

Early researchers recognized that there were inherent features in resilient children and identified temperament as a trait that contributed to resilience in children faced with risks, stating that some children have temperaments that are pro-social and know how to seek help and easily elicit attention from others (Garmezy, 1983; Rutter, 1987; Werner, 1995). Recently literature has emerged that examines the genetic factors or inherent traits that influence resilience (Brendtro & Longhurst, 2005; Kim-Cohen et al., 2004). Brendtro and Longhurst make the assertion that the brain is designed to be resilient and that "resilience is universal across all cultures and encoded in human DNA" (p. 53). They further assert that resilience is using intelligence to overcome challenges and that "best practices with youth at risk" are to provide opportunities for solving problems, strengthening resilience and creating positive bonds with caring adults (p. 58).

Kim-Cohen and colleagues (2004) discuss the genetic influence on resilience as it involves behavioral and cognitive processes and suggest that the same genetic factors that contribute to parental care-giving capacity may contribute to positive adaptation in their children. They conducted a study with 1,116 five-year-old twin pairs, looking at genetic

4

and environmental influences on the resilience of children exposed to deprived economic conditions. They explored the connections between poverty, lack of effective parenting, and children's behavior problems and the process of resilience in response to these problems. They make the assertion that resilience is a "multidimensional construct" with behavior and cognitive components. They describe specific protective factors for different types of resilience and outcomes. Some of the protective variables they describe that contribute to resilience are: child temperament, parent-child relationship with parental warmth toward child and social support for parents. Their research concludes that resilience is in part genetic and "genetic influences may operate by shaping the way children react to misfortune" (p. 663).

Little and colleagues (2004) conclude that " ...a risk factor is something that increases the chance of a specified outcome" (p. 105). They state that children with family risk factors are several times more apt to exhibit antisocial behavior in adolescence than their peers. However, they state that only 4 out of 10 children with serious risk factors become antisocial adolescents. They examined service interventions for children in need, taking into consideration risk, protective factors, resilience and coping. Using poverty as an example, they make the statement that "poverty does not cause childhood needs" and explain that several risk factors interact to create a threat to healthy development in a child (p. 107). Poverty could lead to living in crowded conditions, putting mothers at increased risk for depression that may influence parenting. The impact of the poverty creates an accumulation of risk factors that may have a negative effect on child development. Little and colleagues refer to this as a "causal chain" and state that interventions at various points in the chain may be necessary to break the chain. Some children are more resistant than others to this chain of risks due to protective factors, resilience and coping mechanisms. A protective factor does not eliminate the risk, but helps alleviate the effects.

Little and colleagues (2004) cite recent research that describes resilience as involving "environmental as well as constitutional factors and its strength varies in relation to life domains and stage of development". These authors describe interventions to foster resilience that should include: providing social support of caring adults in the child's life, teaching coping skills, mobilizing the inherent strengths of the child and providing opportunities.

Smokowski (1998) makes suggestions for resilience-based intervention for children at-risk for healthy development. He defines resilience as a "positive adaptation and competence despite the presence of substantial risk" (p. 338). The various types of "risk traits" described are: individual temperament or genetic predisposition to various illnesses that "heighten vulnerability to negative outcomes", environmental conditions that contribute to risk such as indirect ones of neighborhood poverty and high unemployment or direct risks such as inadequate parenting or peer pressure. He states that accumulation of risks can have serious negative effects on the developmental outcome of a child. One of the protective factors suggested by Smokowski for reducing the effects of risks is promoting self-efficacy.

The above researchers have studied children exposed to risk and found that children can overcome the negative life circumstances that may hinder belief in self and affect performance in some or all areas through protective factors in their environment. Protective factors mediate the risk and enhance functioning. They may be inherent in the child or come from the environment. Some inherent protective factors are: temperament, intelligence, gender, good social skills; environmental protective factors may include: good parenting, positive role models, good schools, religious affiliation and caring adults (Brooks, 2006; Garmezy, 1987; Little et al., 2004; Smokowski, 1998; Werner, 1995).

Although children may be exposed to stressful life events or conditions some children possess qualities that protect them from the path of delinquency, low self-esteem and hopelessness that often afflict children who have had to face challenges. Rak and Patterson (1996) state, "It has become commonplace to identify that certain children in this modern, complex society are 'at risk' of failing to succeed in life because of the adversities of their young lives."(p. 368). Long-term studies of resilient children, conducted in an effort to determine what distinguishes them from children of similar backgrounds who succumb to life stressors by displaying signs of juvenile delinquency, social and emotional problems and school failure, found that one of the prevailing factors is the availability of caring, supportive adults in their life (Garmezy, 1983; Howard & Dryden; 1999; Rak & Patterson, 1996; Rutter, 1987; Winfield, 1991).

6

Winfield (1991) states that some children may lack social support and community involvement, that offers an opportunity for growth. Supportive adults can help reduce negative effects by altering the child's perception of the risk situation. Winfield further states that self-concept is enhanced through relationships and "successful completion of tasks" (p. 7) and looks at ways to provide an environment in which children can flourish, offering opportunities and encouragement that would foster resilience. Rak and Patterson (1996) also advocate for structured programs for children that provide environments that welcome a child, offer opportunities, place value on the child and have expectations for the potential of the child.

Rutter (1987) formulated a "buffering hypothesis", indicating that social support of caring adults in a child's life can have a buffering effect that reduces the impact of various stressors. Researchers on long-term studies of vulnerable children identified positive adult role models such as: teachers, school counselors, supervisors of after-school programs, coaches, mental health workers, community center workers, clergy and neighbors as buffers for vulnerable children (Garmezy, 1983; Howard & Dryden, 1999; Rak & Patterson, 1996; Rutter, 1987). They found that "resilient" children often had a host of mentors throughout their childhood.

Supportive adults, acting as role models, have been listed as important protective factors against a child's involvement in risky behavior and ensuring a positive outcome in the lives of children at risk (Benard, 1997; Brooks, 2006; Little et al., 2004; McMillan & Reed, 1994; Werner, 1995; Winfield, 1991). These researchers cite care and support of adults, who hold high expectations for children and provide opportunities for success as paramount in fostering healthy development in children.

Resilience and Self-efficacy

While resilience is the ability to bounce back and persevere in the face of adversity, it is necessary to believe that one has the ability to do this. Self-efficacy is the belief that one has the capability to perform certain tasks, achieve specific goals and face challenges (Bandura, 1977, 1995, 1997). The focal point of Bandura's (1997) social cognitive theory is perceived self-efficacy. Bandura and colleagues (2001) state that self-efficacy governs "resilience to daunting impediments" (p.190). Bandura (1995) uses the term resilience to describe self-efficacy:

" Self-efficacy beliefs are the product of a complex process of self-persuasion that relies on cognitive processing of diverse sources of efficacy information conveyed enactively, vicariously, socially and physiologically" (p.11).

Self-efficacy is explained in detail in the following chapter.

A review of the literature on resilience reveals a connection between self-efficacy and resilience (Bandura, 1995, 1997, 2001; Brooks, 2006; Dubow, Arnett, Smith & Ippolito, 2001; Gilgun, 1996; Harvey & Delfabbro, 1994; Howard & Dryden, 1999; McMillan & Reed, 1994; Smokowski, 1998). Harvey and Delfabbro (2004) acknowledge the association between self-efficacy and resilience and question why Bandura's theory of self-efficacy has not appeared more frequently in resilience research. Rutter (1987) offers a view of the process of protection and the importance of moderating the risk factors. Part of the process described by Rutter is the promotion of self-efficacy through achievements. Rutter states that self-efficacy is a strong predictor of resilience. Examining psychopathology and resilience, Gilgun (1996) found that not all people succumb to childhood risk factors and acknowledged that mediators act to diminish them. Among the mediators expressed are self-efficacy and supportive adult relationships. Smokowski (1998), in describing interventions to target risk factors, states that they should include enhancement of self-efficacy and further asserts that self-efficacy may serve as a protective factor in helping young people face challenging events. Brooks (2006) also describes self-efficacy as a protective factor against risk.

In a 9-month study of inner-city children exposed to chronic stress, Dubow and colleagues (2001) examined variables that contribute to positive expectations in the children. Among these were social support and problem-solving efficacy. These authors state that psychosocial resilience should be the goal of any program to benefit youth at risk for achieving their potential.

McMillan and Reed (1994) looked at students at risk of school dropout and found that those who succeeded despite of the presence of risk factors had a strong sense of self-efficacy. They viewed success as a choice that the students had undertaken and gave credit to their personal effort. Resilience was seen as the outcome of self-efficacy.

Although the studies mentioned suggest a relationship between self-efficacy and resilience, this author has found no empirical evidence to identify a clear association between self-efficacy and resilience. Bandura (1997), the foremost author on self-efficacy, offers the notion that without self-efficacy or the belief that one can act to effect change, there would be no resilience.

According to the body of research presented in this chapter, families are beset with a variety of impediments to childrearing that label their children "at-risk" for failure in achieving essential life goals and engaging in antisocial behavior. We describe these children as being "at risk", for these are problems that may limit the capacity of a child to develop his or her gifts and talents due to their challenging environments. It is not the intention of the research presented here to "fix" or change the child, rather it is intended to foster the child's inherent strengths and talents. The reality is that some conditions are here to stay and children certainly are not to blame for the shortcomings that life has dealt them. Interventions that help young people rise above their circumstances are necessary to protect them from the risk factors that may be present in their environment. Decades of research have shown how a great number of children exposed to a multitude of risks have thrived and overcome adversity (Connell et al., 1994; Garmezy, 1983; Kim-Cohen et al., 2004; Rak & Patterson 1996; Rutter, 1987; Werner & Smith, 1992).

Teaching life skills and enhancing self-efficacy in children may help them overcome some of the challenges they face. The literature has indicated that there is a strong link between childhood resilience and social support (Brown, 2004; Bandura, 1997; Benard, 1991; Brooks, 2006; Garmezy, 1983; Harvey & Delfabbro, 2004; Rak & Patterson, 1996; Rutter, 1987; Werner & Smith, 1992). The literature also shows evidence that self-efficacy is the force behind resilience, the little voice that tells the child he or she has the capability to keep on going (Howard & Dryden, 1999; McMillan & Reed, 1994).

Research Focus

The focus of the research presented in this book was to determine whether children participating in a group mentoring program that provides sources of self-efficacy information and supports the child through the process of achieving a self-selected goal or goals would increase the child's self-efficacy. Bandura's four sources of self-efficacy information: performance accomplishments, vicarious learning, verbal persuasion and interpretation of physiological states were integrated into the group mentoring process for the purpose of this research. Children were offered opportunities to perform and work toward personal goals; vicarious learning was available through the presence of mentors and peers; the mentors and peers offered encouraging feedback; and children were educated on the effects of feelings and physiological reactions when performing tasks. A measure was created to determine the children's perception of experiencing self-efficacy while participating in the group.

This research project focused on examining children's efficacy in their general approach to tasks. Most of the documented research on raising the self-efficacy in children, reviewed here, has been conducted in academic settings, involving academic achievements (Fall & McLeod, 2001; Fasko & Fasko, 1998; Lee, 2001; Schunk & Swartz, 1993; Schunk & Gunn, 2001; Zimmerman & Martinez-Pons, 1990). The present research differs as it was created in a social context rather than an academic setting, with an adult mentor providing the children with the sources of self-efficacy while they interacted with peers in a group setting.

It was anticipated by the author, consistent with the literature presented here, that the care, support and guidance of the mentor, along with the interaction of peers, would provide an opportunity for growth and the enhancement of self-efficacy in the children. If this type of intervention increases self-efficacy in a short amount of time, with a group of children, it may have important implications for social workers, educators and all those who work with children facing challenges in their life.

CHAPTER TWO

Conceptualization of Variables

The underpinning of this study is self-efficacy, which has its roots in Bandura's (1997) social cognitive theory. Bandura places self-efficacy at the core of all human functioning and identifies it as the missing link in understanding human behavior. It is based on the premise that the way people think, believe and feel affects their behavior and the choices they make. From Bandura's theoretical perspective, people are viewed as proactive organisms in their environment and human function a dynamic interplay of personal, behavioral and environmental forces.

Bandura's Theory of Self-efficacy

Bandura (1997) describes four sources that contribute to self-efficacy information. These sources and the manner in which they operate are outlined below:

1. *Mastery experience* is based on appraisal of past experience where success builds efficacy beliefs. A sense of efficacy is obtained through opportunities to master experience and persevering in the face of adversity.

2. *Vicarious experience* occurs through observing others, acting as role models who teach coping strategies and new ways of doing things; watching peers perform successfully, raising the belief that one has the same capabilities.

3. *Verbal persuasion* or performance feedback carries supportive information, indicating that people improved through their own effort and ability, and helps convince them that they have what it takes to succeed.

4. *Physiological and affective states* affect efficacious beliefs. Low self-efficacy diminishes the ability to reduce negative thoughts and emotions. This sometimes creates physical stress. Understanding and reducing stress and correcting negative thoughts through verbal persuasion can improve affective states.

The choices individuals make are based on the judgments they make about their capabilities, which, in turn, are influenced by the four sources of information described above. Thus, the environment and social system of an individual may influence

11

aspirations, emotional states, and self-efficacy beliefs (Bandura, 1977), as self-efficacy is reinforced in several ways, as described above.

The terms "child" or "children" are used in examples throughout this book for the purpose of this research project. However, the same principles may be applied to adults. Within the framework of self-efficacy lie *personal judgment*, in which children judge their capabilities to perform on certain tasks; *domain-specific performance*, or linkage of efficacy beliefs to specific domains of functioning, e.g., a child who judges him or herself as capable of performing well on a math test may doubt his or her ability to perform well on a vocabulary test; *context performance,* where a child may have less efficacy while performing in a competitive setting but feel quite capable performing in a cooperative classroom; and *temporal effect* of performance, where a child rates how he or she expects to performance prior to the task, and success is measured through meeting expectations of mastery (Zimmerman & Martinez-Pons, 1990). Perceptions of self-efficacy also determine how knowledge and skills are acquired, as one will strive toward what one perceives as attainable. A child's efficacy beliefs will determine choice of activity, how much effort the child will expend on the task, the duration of persistence that the child will put forth and how resilient he or she will be in the face of adversity (Bandura, 1997). Children with a high sense of efficacy will "more readily participate, work harder and persist longer" (Zimmerman, 1995, p. 304).

As outlined above, there are four sources that enhance the development of self-efficacy: performance accomplishments, vicarious learning, verbal persuasion and interpretation of physiological states (Bandura, 1977). Bandura asserts that personal performance serves as a gauge for measuring self-efficacy and has the strongest influence on enhancing it. Watching peers or role models perform helps a child to believe that he or she can do it also. Children receive positive persuasive information from teachers, parents, mentors, coaches and peers. Physiological states such as perspiring, heart rate and moods also impact self-efficacy, as people may interpret these reactions as an inability to perform. These four sources do not directly affect self-efficacy; it is the cognitive appraisal of the information provided that informs self-efficacy beliefs. Self-efficacy involves individuals' beliefs of personal capabilities to exercise control over events in their lives and the belief that they are responsible for their accomplishments.

12

Studies conducted with school children demonstrate that at the base of poor performance lie low self-esteem, low self-efficacy, as well as doubt, anxiety, low expectations and lack of personal responsibility (Bandura, Barbaranelli, Caprara & Pastorelli, 2001; Fall & McLeod 2001). The social environment of a child plays a dominant role in the development of perceived self-efficacy by providing opportunities, role models and feedback (Bandura, 1997).

Several authors have looked at strategies to enhance self-efficacy in children and it has been established that children with high self-efficacy not only perform better academically, but behave better (Fall & McLeod, 2001; Fasko & Fasko, 1998; Furstenberg & Rounds, 1995; Lee, 1999, Schunk & Gunn, 2001; Schunk & Swartz 1993; Zimmerman & Martinez-Pons, 1990). Fasko and Fasko state, "…any program for improving academics and reducing problem behavior must address self-efficacy needs." (p. 592). Furstenberg and Rounds cite examples of how social workers can utilize Bandura's four sources of self-efficacy as a tool for social work intervention. They state that social workers already use concepts of self-efficacy "implicitly" and "…propose that social workers become more knowledgeable about self-efficacy and deliberately incorporate this knowledge into their practice" (p. 587).

Self-efficacy has a cumulative effect, as desired outcomes are produced through experiences. Having knowledge and skills does not necessarily assure that a child will use them effectively and be successful. Children differ in their perceived ability to meet academic demands, regardless of their capability. Substantial research (Bandura, 1995; Schunk, 1996; Schunk & Zimmerman, 1997; Zimmerman, 1995; Zimmerman & Martinez-Pons, 1990) has indicated that efficacious beliefs have the greatest impact on performance and success in academic achievement. Bandura (1997) states that it is, "…over and above actual ability" (p.213). When young people hold the belief that anything is possible, they will pursue their goals and have hope for the future. Personal perception of efficacy is the foundation upon which future achievements, adaptation and the development of a child rests (Bandura, 1997).

A Critique of Self-efficacy Theory

A search of the literature has produced two studies that offer a critical assessment of self-efficacy. Erin (2006) questions the ability of self-efficacy to predict performance over time; and a critical discussion on the biases of self-efficacy theory are presented by Franzblau and Moore (2001). Franzblau and Moore make the statement that self-efficacy theory has a "blaming-the-victim approach to social problems" (p. 83). In their critical analysis of self-efficacy theory they report that self-efficacy is an individual strive for control and access to power. They argue that it is culturally biased toward individualism, disregarding ideologies that support collective efforts and coping. They feel blame is placed on the disadvantaged for "dysfunctional thinking" or just not trying hard enough and that self-efficacy theory is "owned" by those who already have the power and social support. They recommend that society "socialize efficacy" and provide a more equal distribution of resources (p. 94).

Some of the research presented in this book differs from the beliefs of Franzblau and Moore's criticism of self-efficacy and demonstrates that disadvantaged people are empowered through enhancement of self-efficacy. Most of the studies presented here are aimed at helping disadvantaged youth build on strengths and increase coping skills. Bandura (1995) does not present self-efficacy as exclusively an individual phenomenon. Self-efficacy is involved in systemic theory, as increasing the self-efficacy of parents, teachers and clinicians can result in an increase in self-efficacy and enhanced performance in children (Jackson, 2000; Jonson-Reid, Davis, Saunders, Williams & Williams, 2005). Bandura talks about collective self-efficacy where a group of people works toward a common goal and efficacy is essential to success. Bandura states that, "Group achievements and social change are rooted in self-efficacy." (1995, p. 34).

Generalized vs. Specific Self-efficacy

Efficacy expectations may differ in dimensions, such as generality. Some experiences create limited expectations, while others may instill a generalized sense of efficacy that extends beyond a specific experience (Bandura, 1977). Although self-efficacy is often domain specific, Bandura (1997) has outlined several ways in which it can generalize across areas of functioning. A child may perceive him or herself as capable of performing dissimilar tasks requiring similar skills that the child has acquired. When children develop coping skills and self-regulatory skills, with the ability to carry out alternative strategies, they may be applied across a variety of domains. For example, a child may use the same skills for different subjects in school, deciding if it works for one area, it may work for others. If effort and perseverance produce results, the child is able to make the connection to other areas of performance. The attainment of success increases self-efficacy beliefs and may be generalized to many areas of functioning. Generality pertains to the transference of efficacy beliefs, not the acquired knowledge (Pajares & Miller, 1994; Zimmerman, 1995).

Comparison of Self-efficacy, Self-concept, Possible Self and Self-esteem

We may ask how the concept of self-efficacy differs from those of self-concept, possible selves or self-esteem. Bandura (1997) makes the assertion that perceived *self-efficacy* is concerned with judgments of personal capability, whereas *self-esteem* is concerned with judgments of self-worth and makes the statement that, "There is no fixed relationship between beliefs about one's capabilities and whether one likes or dislikes oneself." (p. 11). Linnenbrink and Pintrich (2003) state that *self-esteem* is an emotional reaction to a personal accomplishment, which may have positive or negative connotations.

Linnenbrink and Pintrich (2003) claim that like self-efficacy, *self-concept* involves beliefs about competence; but *self-efficacy* is concerned with specific beliefs and *self-concept* more general beliefs about ability to perform. They further state that *self-efficacy* is more "situational" and pertains to achieving a goal and "judgments of efficacy are in reference to this goal" (p. 121). Bandura (1977) views *self-concept* as a way of either valuing or devaluing oneself in various areas of functioning and that the value derives from the "positive or negative self-reactions it generates" (p. 140).

The construct of *possible selves* symbolizes an ideal self that one would like to become (Markus & Nurius, 1986). It also represents the self one is afraid of becoming. *Possible selves* represent hopes, goals, fears and threats and symbolize past and future selves. *Possible selves* are views of the self that have not been verified through experience. However, they can serve as motivators for the future (Markus & Nurius). Although persons may create a variety of possible selves, they are restricted by social and cultural restraints (Linnenbrink & Pintrich, 2003; Markus & Nurius, 1986).

While the constructs of self-concept and possible selves have an influence on some areas of functioning, self-efficacy is more specific and situational and has the potential to predict behavior over a wide range of activities (Bandura, 1997). *Self-*

efficacy involves perceived capability to perform certain tasks, whereas *self-concept* is an evaluation of self, incorporating self-esteem and self-worth (Zimmerman, 1995).

Children with high efficacy beliefs will seek challenges, persist more and achieve more (Bandura, 1977, 1995, 1997). The marked distinction between *self-efficacy* and *self-concept* is the ability of *self-efficacy* to predict outcome and research has supported this concept (Bandura, 1995; Bandura et al., 2001; Pajares & Miller, 1994; Zimmerman, 1995). Perceived *self-efficacy* is pervasive, affecting academic performance, establishment of goals, motivation, perseverance, social behavior, career choices, problem-solving ability and resilience (Bandura et al., 2001; Fall & McLeod, 2001; Fasko & Fasko, 1998; Lee, 1999; Scheel & Rieckmann, 1998; Schunk & Swartz, 1993; Zimmerman, 1995).

Bandura (1997) claims that *self-efficacy* beliefs predict the goals people will choose and the effort they will use to achieve those goals. Self-efficacy can serve as a resource when faced with critical life events or transitions. It is perceived capability to overcome adversity, without adhering to environmental or cultural constraints. Bandura asserts that the predictive qualities of self-efficacy go beyond self-concept, self-esteem or possible self.

Self-efficacy and Mentoring

The positive effect of supportive adults has been instrumental in enhancing self-efficacy in children (Brooks, 2006; Garmezy, 1993; Howard & Dryden, 1999; Little et al., 2004; Smokowski, 1998; Werner, 1995). The construct of self-efficacy is utilized in this book to describe the degree to which children view themselves as capable of performing age-appropriate tasks such as schoolwork, getting along with siblings and peers, behaving in the classroom and the extent to which they measure their sense of competency in achieving goals related to these tasks. While interventions with children at risk have posed a challenge to social workers, the concept of building on children's self-efficacy beliefs has brought hope for positive outcomes and creates an atmosphere of optimism for children who may lack the benefits necessary for healthy development. It provides a chance for those who work with them to foster such development.

Enhancing self-efficacy inspires children to believe that their efforts and determination can make things possible. This may be achieved within a supportive environment that offers opportunities to set and achieve goals through the social support of mentors and peers; to experience vicarious learning; to receive verbal persuasion; and to understanding the effect of physiological states on performance.

Introducing a supportive adult into the life of a child through a formal mentoring program may provide opportunities and experiences for enhancing self-efficacious beliefs by offering support, guidance and role modeling as the child develops personal responsibility, goal direction, determination, positive attitude, confidence, problem-solving skills and self-respect.

Mentor

The concept of a mentor comes to us from Greek mythology. In Homer's poem, *The Odyssey*, Odysseus requested that his friend Mentor take charge of his son while he went off to war in Troy (McCluskey, Noller, Lamoureaux & McCluskey, 2004). The authors list three responsibilities of a mentor: continuing to carry out duties while assuming a caregiver role, serving as a conduit for the wisdom of others and developing a long-term connection.

A mentor is described as someone older than the child who may provide a bonding experience, serve as a role model, offer opportunities, provide encouragement, guidance and facilitate a sense of competence (Terry, 1999; Rhodes, 1994). Rhodes says a mentor is a person "...aimed at developing the competence and character of the protégé" and the relationship as one that "...facilitates the child's transition into adulthood" (pp. 188-189). The presence of such a figure in the life of a child at risk provides the child with opportunity for growth and development, lends support and bolsters self-efficacy. Mentors may be formal or informal. Formal mentors are usually assigned through a mentoring program and informal mentor/mentee relationships are generally formed through the child's social network, with someone familiar with the child such as a relative, neighbor, teacher, coach etc.

Terry (1999) describes mentoring as a "successful approach to meet students' individual needs" (p.237). Mentors can play a pivotal role in the lives of disadvantaged youth, as underprivileged children may lack supportive role models who can be instrumental to healthy normal development (Alessandri & Keating 1995; Lee, 1999; Barron-McKeagney, Woody, & D'Souza, 2000; Rhodes, 1994; Terry, 1999).

17

The mentor-child relationship has the potential to strengthen character, help the child face stressful life events and overcome adversity by instilling a sense of personal competency and optimism. A mentor offers young people, who may not have many advantages, hope for a brighter and more productive future, as it has been firmly established that mentors have been identified as a vital source of social support and contribute greatly to the social growth of children by fostering the acquisition of social and cognitive skills, enhancing pro-social behavior and reducing delinquency (Benard, 1993; Fishman & Stelk, 1997; Lee, 1999; Rak & Patterson, 1996; Rhodes, 1994; Terry, 1999; Townsel, 1997).

As the literature presented here demonstrates, a relationship with a caring adult who provides encouragement and serves as a healthy role model can protect young people from negative environmental influences and play a role in their development into responsible adults. Children may have one or more existing mentors in their life.

Mentoring Programs

There is a small, but noteworthy, body of research examining the positive effects of mentoring programs on children (Alessandri & Keating, 1995; Baron-McKeagney et al., 2000; Rhodes, 1994; Terry, 1999).

Alessandri and Keating (1995) conducted a study measuring the effectiveness of a mentoring program for at-risk youth, including 34 experimental and 34 control subjects. The results indicated that mentored children increased their self-concept significantly as opposed to the non-mentored children. Another study found that a formal mentoring program did improve the aspirations of young people resulting in greater interest in school, academic improvement and expanding future goals (Lee, 1999). Baron-McKeagney and colleagues (2000) targeted 10-year olds in an at-risk neighborhood and provided 18 months of mentoring, focusing on social skills training. They report the program was successful in improving child self-concept, social skills enhancement and reduction of problem behaviors. Rhodes (1994), in a review of the mentoring literature, validates the benefits of supportive adults in the lives of disadvantaged youth and the role they play in bolstering the resilience in these young people. Terry (1999) examined a community/school mentoring program for elementary students and had positive feedback

18

from parents and teachers on grades, effort, behavior and enhancement of self-confidence, although no formal measures were taken.

The above research investigations cite the positive effects of mentoring children, such as improved self-concept; academic success; self-efficacy; increased aspiration; prevention of delinquency; social competence, and the fostering of resilience. Serving as role models, mentors help provide protective factors against adversity that the child may face and assist the child in synthesizing stressful events; thus modifying the negative impact on development by instilling a sense of competence.

Rhodes (1994) raises some important issues to take into consideration when examining mentor relationships. Some of these are: whether a mentor relationship actually promotes resilience, or whether resilient children are more apt to seek out mentors; the training of mentors which may be limited; failed relationships that can lead to "hurt and disappointment"; the difference and advantages/disadvantages between two types of mentorships, assigned and those developing within the child's social support network; the factors that motivate mentors; and the benefits they derive from the relationship. In the research presented in this book, the mentors were assigned and trained and contracted to fulfill their obligation for the duration of the program.

The Process of Mentoring

The philosophy behind mentoring is for adults to offer a positive attitude toward the development of youth. Baron-McKeagney and colleagues (2000) describe mentoring as "a process aimed at strengthening an individual at risk through a personal relationship with an experienced and caring person. Through shared activities, guidance, information and encouragement, the individual gains in character and competence and begins setting positive life goals." (p. 40). These researchers state that one of the psychological changes that takes place in the process is empowerment, which increases self-efficacy. Although mentors cannot change the environment of the child, they can add a social dimension to the child's life, ultimately increasing the social competence necessary for healthy development and success.

During the mentoring process an adult provides a child with opportunities, support and the guidance vital to reaching his or her potential. A number of authors link mentoring to a decrease in juvenile delinquency (Brown, 2004; Barron-McKeagney et al.,

19

2000; Benard, 1997; Lee, 1999; Rak & Patterson, 1996). Several researchers offer theoretical explanations for the mentoring process. Barron-McKeagney and colleagues cite two theories, social network theory and social learning theory, and explain that by expanding the social network of a child and exposing the child to the larger community, without losing their cultural connection and identity, mentors can "offer access to new goals, ideas, and resources" (p. 40). Lee views mentoring in the light of social capital theory and states, "a mentoring relationship constitutes a social capital that is critical to human development, because it enables students to develop the necessary attitudes, effort, and conception of self that they need to succeed in school and as adults." (p. 171). Lee also explains mentoring in terms of social learning theory, which "has postulated that humans tend to emulate the behavior they see in others they care for and admire. From this perspective, formal mentoring programs establish the critical one-on-one relationship with a caring adult, which supports the healthy development of youth" (p. 172).

Mentoring helps children gain the life skills they need to succeed. One of the aspects that influence human performance is perceived competence. Lee (1999) explains that human performance may be positively influenced by belief systems. Enhancing children's belief system through mentoring programs can "teach them the efficacy of effective effort; provide them access to and acquaint them with values, resources and people of different occupational and social worlds; and instill dreams and visions about their lives and their futures in order to motivate them toward successful upward mobility in society" (p. 41).

Brown applauds the mentoring process but makes the statement that "What works for one client may not work for another..." (p. 76). He speaks from personal experience and claims that troubled youth who have the opportunity to work with a role model "increase their chance to be resilient" (p. 78). Brown believes that the "collective effort" of others like himself who have beat the odds can have important implications for helping children at risk.

Models of Mentoring

Mentoring has earned much public recognition and popularity for its success in contributing to the positive development of youth. In reviewing the literature, the traditional type, one child paired with an adult, is the type most frequently cited.

However, as this form of providing positive development for youth became increasingly popular, various forms of mentoring have emerged beyond the traditional method. Some of these types are short-term, long-term, team mentoring and group mentoring. The model of mentoring utilized for the research presented in this book is group mentoring. This type of mentoring was used for several reasons: it provides an intervention to many children at one time; it offers the children the opportunity to interact with peers in a social setting; and having a number of children participating, makes it more plausible to measure the effects of the mentor/child interaction.

Group mentoring takes place when an adult volunteer works with a group of children. Groups may be co-facilitated. A Girl Scout troop is now considered to be a mentoring group (Saito & Blyth, 1992). Although one-on-one mentoring is the most widely used model, group mentoring is becoming increasingly popular for some very practical reasons. It is cost-effective, as it can serve a number of children at one time and generally takes place in a school, reaching many at-risk youth who may have difficulty signing up for traditional mentors. Most mentoring groups are also structured groups with planned activities and goals. (Herrera,Vang, & Gale, 2002; Rhodes, Grossman & Roffman, 2002; Saito & Blyth, 1992). Rhodes states that nearly 70% of mentoring programs take place in schools. These researchers express the advantage of children being in a familiar site.

Group mentoring is beneficial to the child participants as it provides the opportunity for interacting with peers in the company of supportive adults, thus offering an opportunity for vicarious learning and improved social skills; it provides the mentoring experience to youth who may not feel comfortable in a one-on-one relationship; and it promotes positive peer interactions (Herrera et al., 2002; Saito & Blyth, 1992; Mitchell, 1999; Rhodes et al., 2002). A search of the literature revealed that there is very little research available regarding group mentoring. Some of the concerns with this model of mentoring are confidentiality, negative interactions among youth, lack of individual attention, mentors favoring some children over others and lack of time spent with mentor (Rhodes et al.; Herrera et al., 2002). However there is insufficient research to support this evidence.

In an investigation of three group-mentoring programs, Herrera and colleagues (2002) state that the most beneficial aspect of group mentoring is the improvement of social skills and attribute this to "adult guidance in the context of peer interactions" (p. 45). Positive peer relationships extended outside of the group and may be an important implication for future success. They also found that the mentored group had enhanced academic performance and positive attitude toward schoolwork. Although group-mentor relationships are not usually as intense as one-on-one mentor/mentee relationships, the research of Herrera and colleagues (2002) showed that some children did form close relationships with the mentor in the group. These intimate relationships were attributed to a mentor's regular group attendance, sensitivity to youth interests and needs and encouraging one-on-one conversations.

A study to examine the nature of mentoring relationships was conducted by Saito and Blyth (1992). These investigators explored and documented the various types of mentoring. Among them was group mentoring. The mentoring program contributing to the study served 32 elementary schools, with 93 co-leaders among the groups. The mentors were trained in a nine-session program and provided with a guide. The goal of the mentoring groups was to help children get along better with each other. The mentees talked about problems they were having and received feedback about their behavior and attitude from the mentors. Program participants reported positive outcomes for the children who participated in the study.

Although the research on group mentoring is sparse, Herrera and colleagues (2002) and Saito and Blyth (1992) have conducted large studies which yield positive results and found that group mentoring provides a safe place for self-expression, improved social skills and peer interactions, improved communication, enhanced academic performance and attitude toward studies. Group success is attributed to the interactive role of child, mentors and group. Saito and Blyth make the statement:

> "What is perhaps the most important finding of this study is that, regardless of the type of mentoring program, mentoring is a win-win situation ... Young people win; adult volunteers win. It is, quite frankly, society at large that is eventually the real winner." (p. 62).

22

CHAPTER THREE

Review of the Literature

This chapter will explain the two major variables in this book: self-efficacy and mentoring. The empirical studies relating to these variables will be reviewed. The range of mentoring models will be presented.

Self-efficacy and Education

Much of the research on self-efficacy in children has been performed in academic settings and supports the link between self-efficacy and academic progress (Bandura et al., 1996; Fall & McLeod, 1991; Holden, Wade, Mitchel, Ewart & Islam, 1998; Jonson-Reid et al., 2005; Lee, 1999; Linnenbrink & Pintrich, 2003; Schunk & Swartz, 1993; Rak & Patterson, 1996; Shih & Alexander, 2000; Zimmerman, 1995). Schools bear the responsibility of educating and socializing children and serve as an environment for cultivating self-efficacy.

Self-efficacy beliefs on academic functioning, meaning children believe they have the ability to regulate their own learning, will determine academic success (Bandura et al., 1996). Bandura's social cognitive theory explains the influence environmental factors have on a child's development. He states that, "…personal agency operates within a broad network of sociostructural and psychosocial influences in which efficacy beliefs play an influential regulative function" (p. 1207). Within this sociostructural framework, the socioeconomic status of the family, parent academic efficacy, peer influence and "self processes" all contribute to the academic efficacy, aspirations and achievement of the child. The child with a solid sense of perceived self-efficacy will set higher goals and have a firmer commitment to them.

The research results of Bandura and colleagues (1996) demonstrate that parents' belief in the efficacy to promote their children's academic achievement leads to high academic efficacy in children which is generally accompanied by 'prosocialness, peer acceptance, low despondency, repudiation of moral disengagement, a low level of emotional and behavioral problems and high scholastic achievement'. This research also supported the notion that perceived self-regulatory efficacy was related to academic success and takes into consideration the influence of psychosocial factors on self-efficacy beliefs and the importance of parental efficacy for assisting in the educational development of their children.

Linnenbrink and Pintrich (2003) view self-efficacy as a key construct in students' motivation to learn and cite empirical evidence for the predictive power of self-efficacy. A child's judgment of capability encourages engagement and learning in the classroom, as the child who believes s/he can do it, will persist longer, put more effort into a task and use cognitive strategies to achieve a goal. Self-efficacy beliefs will determine the quantity and quality of effort put forth (Pintrich & De Groot, 1990). Linnenbrink and Pintrich find it prudent to incorporate self-efficacy enhancement in the classroom and offer some suggestions for teachers. Some of these suggestions are: providing accurate feedback to help students develop reasonable efficacy beliefs; providing challenging, but attainable academic tasks and conveying to the students that they believe they are capable. These researchers have strong convictions that classroom teachers can be instrumental in enhancing the self-efficacy of their students.

Zimmerman (1995) examines the role of self-efficacy on educational development, as efficacy beliefs have an impact on motivation to learn, affective response to effort and academic attainment. Children with high self-efficacy for self-regulatory learning will take responsibility for their own progress and thus play a proactive role in regulating their own learning. Zimmerman and Martinez-Pons (1990) demonstrated this concept in a study of 45 boys and 45 girls from 5th, 8th, and 11th grades. The findings yield support for their hypothesis that level of verbal and math self-efficacy would predict use of students' self-regulatory learning strategies. These efficacy beliefs are essential to future success, as self-regulated learners will pursue intellectual paths and have higher career aspirations (Bandura et al., 1996). In contrast, Bandura and colleagues assert that those with low efficacy to meet academic demands through their own regulation of learning will become anxious, prone to failure and experience a diminished sense of efficacy.

Fall (1999) looked at the relationship between a play therapy intervention and the self-efficacy of the child participants as it pertained to coping behaviors and academic achievement. A counselor saw sixty-two children from kindergarten through third grade once a week for six weeks for individual play therapy. The results indicated a significant increase in self-efficacy based on teachers' ratings for the experimental group.

Fall and McLeod (2001) were concerned with identifying children with low self-efficacy in an effort to provide interventions to raise their self-efficacy, in an attempt to improve academic functioning. After conducting research with 267 preschool through sixth grade students from rural school districts, Fall and McLeod (2001) make several suggestions for raising the self-efficacy of children who have demonstrated a low level. Some of these implications are: using a child's self-efficacy information when handling children with behavior problems; modeling behavior for children and providing them with performance feedback; acknowledging effort through use of verbal reflections; and assigning attainable tasks. Fall (2001) developed the self-efficacy scales that were utilized in the research presented in this book. The scales have been advantageous as they may be applied in a short amount of time, have established a relationship between self-efficacy and intervention and have construct validity.

In looking at programs that build self-esteem and those designed to enhance self-efficacy, Jonson-Reid and colleagues (2005) found that self-efficacy had a stronger connection to academic performance than self-esteem. Seeking to help understand academic self-efficacy and African-American youths, to augment school social work practice with that population, they found that verbal encouragement in the form of positive feedback statements and role models were significant contributors to self-efficacy in the young people they observed.

Schunk and Gunn (1986) conducted a study to determine whether the use of children's task strategies to solve division problems had an impact on self-efficacy and skills. Fifty elementary students, selected by teachers for their inability to solve the math problems, were used as a sample. This study also sought to determine if children's attributions influenced self-efficacy and skills. The children were given a pre-test and post-test for self-efficacy in solving division problems. Between tests, they received math instructions. Prior to the last training sessions, children's attributions for solving problems were measured. This research showed that performing a task well did not necessarily increase self-efficacy, as personal self-efficacy is judged by cognitive appraisal of performance. The findings suggest that ability attributes have a stronger impact on performance appraisal than effort. It is suggested that when providing performance feedback, teachers put emphasis on ability rather than effort, utilizing statements such as, "You're good at that", rather than, "You're working hard" (Schunk & Gunn, 1986, p.243).

The research reviewed here supports the relationship between efficacy beliefs and performance and offers suggestions for educators to enhance self-efficacy in children. It also demonstrates an association between self-efficacy and pro-social behavior, making the claim that children who believe they are capable will perform better in all realms.

Self-efficacy and Goals

The research studies reviewed here were conducted in academic settings, examining the effects of goal setting on the self-efficacy of children and have offered positive results (Bandura, 1986; Bandura & Schunk, 1981; Patrick, Hicks & Ryan, 1997; Schunk, 1996, 1995, 1985; Schunk & Swartz, 1993; Schunk & Zimmerman, 1997; Shih & Alexander, 2000). Bandura (1986) stresses the importance of goal setting on motivation and performance and the role self-efficacy plays in working toward goals.

Bandura (1995) postulates that self-efficacy determines the goals a child will choose, the effort she or he will expend on the goals and the persistence that will be put forth to achieve the goal. Goal setting is "…influenced by self-appraisal of capabilities … the stronger sense of efficacy the greater degree of goal challenges and stronger commitment to goals" (p.6). Efficacy beliefs play a key role in the goals selected and the commitment to those goals. Children will set goals that they feel they are capable of performing.

A good deal of the empirical research on goals and self-efficacy in children has been conducted by Schunk and colleagues (1997; 1996; 1995; 1993; 1986; 1985; 1983) and pertains to learning goals, or mastering the process involved in performing academic tasks. The empirical studies reviewed here indicate that goal setting and feedback on progress do have a positive impact on the self-efficacy of grade school children. As children establish goals for themselves and work toward those goals, they gain a sense of competency and self-efficacy is heightened. When they approach tasks, they will have a specific goal in mind and evaluate their own performance.

Schunk (1985) maintains that goal setting increases motivation and bolsters perseverance. He describes the core properties of goals as: specificity, difficulty level and proximity. Specific goals lead to better performance than general goals. Children perform better if they have the ability to attain their set goal. Goals that can be achieved in the near rather than distant future will evoke increased motivation. Schunk postulated that children who set their own goals would develop a higher level of self-efficacy and skills through the process of goal achievement. In studying sixth grade students with learning disabilities, comparing children with self-set goals to those with assigned goals, Schunk discovered that the children who set their own goals enhanced their self-efficacy and skills as evidenced by the post-test scores. The study supports the self-efficacy research demonstrating that self-efficacy is enhanced through successful performance and continues to build on subsequent achievement. It suggests goal setting may serve as a useful intervention for enhancing the self-efficacy of children.

Schunk (1990) states, "Self-efficacy and goal setting are affected by self observation, self-judgment and self-reaction." (p. 72). Goal setting heightens the learning process, thus children become self-regulated learners. Self-regulated learning occurs when a child sets a goal, persists in achieving that goal, holding the belief that s/he will reach the desired outcome. A goal is something the child is consciously trying to accomplish. As perceived capability is strengthened and the present goal is achieved, the child will set new goals and continue to learn and be challenged (Schunk & Swartz, 1993).

Schunk and Swartz (1993) looked at 33 academically gifted fourth grade students and the effects of strategy goals and feedback on self-efficacy during a writing assignment. The children were tested on self-efficacy through perceived capabilities with writing tasks. They were randomly assigned to three groups. Each group received instructions, but only one group received feedback as they progressed. The results indicated that children receiving a strategy goal and progress feedback enhanced achievement and perceptions of efficacy. This study also demonstrated a relationship between self-efficacy and skill, influenced by performance, but the children who received strategy goals with feedback on their progress throughout performance demonstrated the highest level of self-efficacy. This offers helpful suggestions for raising self-efficacy through goal strategies and feedback.

Shih and Alexander (2000) assessed the relationship between self-efficacy beliefs and setting personal goals for fraction skills with 84 fourth-grade Taiwanese students. The students were randomly assigned to goal setting vs. non-goal setting and self-referenced vs. social-referenced feedback. There was no difference between the children in the goal setting and non-goal setting groups. However, self-referenced was significantly more beneficial than social referenced feedback in enhancing both self-efficacy and fraction skills. Schunk (1990) and Zimmerman (1989) have found that goal setting leads to increased learning, perseverance and strategy planning. Shih and Alexander (2000) established that this type of self-regulatory learning has implications for development of self-efficacy in the students and attribute the lack of relationship between goal setting and self-efficacy to classroom situations and "culturally induced differences" (p. 542).

Patrick and Hicks (1997) conducted a survey with 753 fifth-grade students, looking at the relationship between students' perceived academic efficacy, social efficacy and social goals. It was predicted that children who were able to fulfill the social standards of their classroom should also be able to meet the academic demands. The findings indicated that students' efficacy beliefs about their academic ability was significantly related to their efficacy to relate to others and their goals to be socially responsible by adhering to classroom norms. It emphasizes the relationship between social efficacy, social goals and academic efficacy and underlines the importance of social relationships in the classroom, with both teachers and peers, in promoting academic success.

Goal attainment raises the level of self-efficacy and the sense of competence that children feel. Increasing self-efficacy has a positive affect on the type of goals that children will set for the future, the effort they will be put into those goals and the rate of perseverance they will exert.

Self-efficacy and Careers

Career aspirations and pursuits are formed in the early years and are influenced by judgments about capabilities. Bandura and colleagues (1996) have hailed the predictive power of self-efficacy in determining career choices. They state that efficacious beliefs above academic performance are the strongest predictor in the trajectories that children will choose – "Unless people believe that they can produce desired effects by their actions, they have little incentive to act" (Bandura et al., 1996, p.1206). Perceived self-efficacy to pursue educational requirements and occupational roles affects the career choices a person will make. People generally do not choose careers that they perceive to be beyond their capabilities. Options are based on their belief in ability to acquire the knowledge and perform the skills necessary to fulfill a given role. Those with high efficacy beliefs in their ability to perform will welcome challenge. They have more options for career choices, job attainment and satisfaction which have a great impact on lifestyle and quality of life, as those who feel capable and effective are less prone to stress and depression (Bandura et al., 1996).

The role of self-efficacy in career decisions has been empirically explored and the research indicates a staunch connection between self-efficacy beliefs and vocational choices (Bandura et al., 2001; Brown, 1999; Clement, 1987; Gillespie & Hillman, 1993; Hackett, 1995). These authors reveal that career self-efficacy of youth will predict the occupations that they choose and that self-efficacy beliefs are strengthened through performance accomplishments.

Hackett (1995) maintains that career choice is one of the most important decisions of human functioning and that "work adjustment is intimately associated with mental health and physical well-being" (p. 232). Hackett elucidates Bandura's self-efficacy theory while explaining career development as outlined in the literature on women's career choices and pursuits. Hackett and Betz (1981) assert that traditional female upbringing hinders the development of occupational efficacy beliefs of women, thus limiting their career choices. Gender may inhibit the kinds of experiences that females have which impact on the development of self-efficacy beliefs for occupation. An exploration of the literature on career self-efficacy of youth confirms the relationship between career self-efficacy and occupational choice (Clement, 1987; Gillespie & Hillman, 1993; Hackett, 1995). Hackett advocates for the enhancement of efficacy beliefs in women and minorities to expand career aspirations and affirms that the four sources of efficacy information – mastery performance, vicarious learning, verbal persuasion and physiological states – may be used remedially to correct negative efficacy beliefs. Hackett (p. 253) states, "...we must not forget the role of self-efficacy in generating options and creating opportunities" when working with youth.

In a study conducted by Clement (1987) of 121 pre-university and university male and female students testing their self-efficacy for entering traditional male or female occupations, it was discovered that females had lower self-efficacy than males for all but one of traditional male careers; males did not lack self-efficacy toward entering traditional female occupational roles. In contrast to the contentions of Hackett (1995), Clement found that low self-efficacy of woman did not prevent them from pursuing traditional male occupations. Bandura and colleagues (2001), in a study with 272 children, looking at the sociocognitive factors that affect children's career aspirations, found that children's academic, social and self-regulatory efficacy predicted career choices. Children chose careers that matched their academic strengths. Traditional gender roles emerged through the career preferences of boys and girls.

Gillespie and Hillman (1993) explored the impact of self-efficacy features on the career choices of 225 high school students, both in general and special educational tracts. This study was concerned with a population 'at-risk' for vocational success. Information was collected through an occupational self-efficacy scale, career decision-making self-efficacy scale and career decision scale. Gender considerations surfaced for occupational choice and self-efficacy for successful job performance, however, males were less apt to consider cross gender roles than females. Males and females scored higher on their respective gender-dominated positions. This study also found that as self-efficacy for carrying out career-related tasks increased, decision making for careers also increased. Students representing the general education populations held higher self-efficacy beliefs than the alternative students or special education students, who had the lowest sense of self-efficacy (Gillespie & Hillman, 1993). This research suggests that 'at risk' students would benefit from developing skills that would enhance their self-efficacy.

The effect of performance accomplishments and vicarious learning experiences on math self-efficacy was measured for college students who were indecisive in their career choice to determine if a combination of both performance accomplishments and vicarious learning would raise the math/science self-efficacy and lead students into career choices in those areas (Brown, 1999). Results demonstrated that the combination of performance accomplishment and vicarious learning had a significant impact on math/science self-efficacy and promotion of career choices in those fields of interest. The performance accomplishment intervention was stronger than the vicarious learning only one. The results of this study indicate that intervention can enhance the self-efficacy for math and science and has important implications for modifying self-efficacy in other domains of functioning.

Brown (1999) emphasizes that self-efficacy is learned and therefore students can be assisted in increasing their self-efficacy beliefs. She identifies three strategies for helping young people develop efficacy expectations that lead to occupational goals. They are: contextual learning, problem-based learning, community-based learning, achievement through proper coaching, and mentoring. Brown emphasizes that particular attention is needed for students with barriers, whether perceived or real, to self-efficacy development due to "poverty, cultural obstacles, or linguistic barriers to career development" (p. 101).

The information provided here demonstrates consistent evidence to confirm the notion that self-efficacy beliefs have the capacity to influence career pursuits. The researchers have also described interventions designed to enhance the self-efficacy for decision-making and career choices (Brown, 1999; Clement, 1987; Gillespie & Hillman, 1993; Hackett, 1995).

Social Work and Self-efficacy

An interest in self-efficacy intervention research is fairly new to the social work profession. The theoretical and empirical support of this construct appearing in the social work literature has focused on health related issues, the effects of social work education on self-efficacy, parenting self-efficacy, the effect of self-efficacy on resilience and self-efficacy intervention (Alter, 1996; Gilgun, 1996; Holden et al., 1998; Holden, Meenaghan, Anastas & Metrey, 2002; Jackson, 2000; Kwok & Wong, 2000; Palmer, 1997; Rosenfeld, Richman & Bowen, 2000; Schofield & Brown, 1999). Holden and colleagues (1998) describe self-efficacy as "a construct consonant with social work values, social work educational traditions and a strengths perspective" (p.129).

31

Furstenberg and Rounds (1995) surmise that social workers inadvertently use self-efficacy sources in their practice. They state, "Social workers' actions and behaviors send messages to clients about their capabilities." (p. 592), and they offer suggestions as to how social workers may purposely integrate the four sources of self-efficacy into their work with clients by becoming more aware of them. This supports a strengths-based model of intervention as it facilitates a person's belief in his or her capability to achieve certain goals through their own effort. When performance is interpreted as being the direct result of one's own capability, self-efficacy is enhanced (Bandura, 1995).

Social workers have incorporated self-efficacy into their work through strengthening a client's belief in competency. Furstenberg and Rounds (1995) state, "Social workers can consciously select from among several channels to increase clients' self-efficacy" (p. 587). They suggest that guidelines for intervention may be based on Bandura's four sources of self-efficacy: enactive attainments, vicarious experience, verbal persuasion and observations of one's own physiological state. Some of these methods are modeling, providing verbal support or 'persuasion', interpreting clients' physiological states, teaching, incorporating new skills, providing feedback, building on clients' strengths and capabilities.

There is a substantial body of research attesting to the validity of education and field practice enhancing self-efficacy and the ability to carry out social work practice, research and technology more effectively (Holden et al., 2002; Holden et al, 1998; Montcalm, 1999; Williams, King & Koob, 2002). Parenting has also become an important area of study in the social work literature, linking self-efficacy to effective parenting, parenting satisfaction, less maternal stress and depression, more sociable and better behaved children (Jackson, 2000; Jackson & Huang, 2000; Coleman & Karraker, 2000; Scheel & Rieckmann, 1998).

Self-efficacy and Resilience

Bandura (1997) looks at self-efficacy as the foundation for resilience. People with a high sense of efficacy quickly bounce back following impediments, as self-efficacy provides the source of persuasion necessary to keep going. Bandura asserts that when faced with adversity, self-efficacy beliefs are resilient and sees them as contributing to the strength of each other. He further explains that the experience of overcoming obstacles bolsters self-efficacy beliefs and these firmly established beliefs of personal capability provide a resilient sense of efficacy that can hold up over time and predict coping behavior. Werner (1992) has performed longitudinal studies of children faced with multiple risk factors and the resilience they display. She reports that a sense of control over one's life circumstances is an important component of resilience. Believing that one has the ability to meet challenges in the face of adversity is based on efficacy beliefs that contribute to resilience (Bandura & Locke, 2003). In a study of social work with teenagers, designed to develop trust in adolescent girls in crisis, Schofield and Brown (1999) describe self-efficacy as a necessary ingredient for resilience and successful relationships. Without the belief that one can persevere and achieve desired outcomes, there is no incentive to act (Bandura, 1995).

Mentoring

The following is a review of the empirical findings that relate to self-efficacy and mentoring. In the research presented here, goal achievement is facilitated through the help of a mentor in a group setting.

Although there are few empirical studies exploring the effects of mentoring on the developmental outcome of young people, Rhodes (1994) makes the statement that "…mentor relationships have been identified as contributing to resilience in high-risk youth" (p. 187). She credits extensive studies of Werner and Smith (1995; 1992) for validating the positive effect that mentors have on healthy development. Based on qualitative investigations, the positive effects of mentors on the lives of disadvantaged children have been cited throughout the mentoring literature (Barron-McKeagney et al., 2000; Benard, 1997; Gilligan, 1999; Katz, 1997; Keating, 1995; Lee, 1999; Rhodes, 1994; Townsel, 1997).

The consistent support and guidance of an adult who values the child can be instrumental in changing the life course of a child at risk. The relationship with a mentor challenges the child's attitudes and belief system, while valuing uniqueness and offering hope. A mentor's faith in the child can help the child to overcome adversity (Katz, 1997).

Townsel (1997) stipulates that identifying qualities of resiliency in a child is one of the "elements of successful mentoring". The author proceeds to state that children

33

live up to adult expectations, whether negative or positive, and stresses the importance of adhering to a philosophy that promotes resiliency in at-risk children. Resilience is viewed as an asset that provides endurance in the face of adversity. The author makes the statement, "...the key element for the successful survivor is the moving from fear to the power and pride of feeling competent. Through recognition of resilience, children can change their lives" (p. 126).

Lee (1999) cites the heightened optimism created by the mentoring literature, looking at the positive effects that mentoring has on self-efficacy and offering hope for disadvantaged youths in reaching their potential. The study, aimed at changing belief systems and promoting upward mobility, looked at 130 elementary and secondary students from disadvantaged family backgrounds. Various theoretical perspectives were utilized to explain the mentoring process, including Bandura's social learning theory. It is suggested that a need exists for further investigation into the effects of mentoring on the self-efficacy of disadvantaged elementary school children to determine the critical components of success. The research presented here will look at elementary school children to determine if the intervention of a mentoring program enhances the self-efficacy of the child participants.

There is no evidence that studies to date have addressed the impact that group mentoring, through the process of achieving a goal, has on the self-efficacy of children. The research presented in this book maintains the belief that when adults have faith in the capabilities of children, provide opportunities for mastery experience, act as role models, give positive verbal feedback and help eliminate negative emotional reactions to stress and self-doubt, self-efficacy is enhanced.

Group Mentoring

With more children growing up in single-parent homes with low incomes and often unsafe neighborhoods, there is an increasing need for positive adult role models. However, there is a shortage of volunteers available as mentors. In an effort to meet the needs of children, mentoring programs have become more diversified to include group mentoring. In a Public/Private Ventures survey of seven hundred mentoring group programs, 20 percent were considered group-mentoring programs (Rhodes, Grossman & Roffman, 2002).

34

Although this type of mentoring relationship may not provide the intimacy and attention of a one-on-one mentor relationship, it can still be a rewarding experience in which a caring adult provides the child, as part of a group, with guidance, instruction and encouragement. It also offers the child the opportunity to socialize with peers, elicit adult support and enhance social skills.

If this study confirms the hypothesis that mentoring programs, focused on goal achievement and teaching life skills, increase the perceived self-efficacy of the child participants, it may serve as a resource for preventive interventions with children utilizing a strength-based model. This could encourage the use of self-efficacy principles for all professionals that work with young people in an effort to assist them in reaching their potential.

CHAPTER FOUR

Methodology

The research presented in this book assesses the relationship between a group mentoring program and the perceived self-efficacy of elementary-school children. This section states the hypotheses and describes the sample, study sites, operational definition of variables, procedures, demographics, measures and data analysis. Finally, limitations of the study are outlined.

Hypotheses

The purpose of this research was to investigate whether participation in a goal-oriented, group-mentoring program would enhance the self-efficacy of the child participants. The investigation was designed to test the following hypotheses:

1. Children participating in the mentoring program will demonstrate a significant increase in perceived self-efficacy scores from pre-test to post-test on the Self-efficacy Scale Student Version (SES-SV).
2. Children participating in the mentoring program will demonstrate significantly higher SES-SV scores at post-test than children in the control group.
3. Children participating in the mentoring program will demonstrate a significant increase in Self-efficacy Scale Teacher Version (SES-TV) scores from pre-test to post-test.
4. Children participating in the mentoring program will demonstrate significantly higher scores on the SES-TV post-test than children in the control group.

In addition to these four hypotheses, this research will look at other variables that may have an impact on self-efficacy such as gender and age of child. It will also assess the results of the Child Rating Scale to determine whether children perceived themselves as having experienced the sources of self-efficacy.

Sample

This was a convenience sample of participants recruited from after-school programs conducted in five urban Catholic schools. Criteria for a child's participation in the study included: being between age 7 and 12 and having no serious learning, emotional or behavioral problems. The ethnic backgrounds of the children that

36

participated in this research are outlined in Table 1 below. Table 2 (p. 38) displays ethnic data according to school.

The total number of children participating was 109, with 63 in the experimental group (31 girls and 32 boys) and 46 in the control group (27 girls and 19 boys). They ranged in age from 8 to 12 years, with a mean age of 9.9 and a mode of 9 years. Other than age, grade and gender, the demographic information was not complete for the entire sample, with 65% of the participants returning the data forms. The 71 children from whom demographic data was obtained are comprised of 32 Hispanic, 25 African-American, 7 Asian, 5 white, one Native American and one other. Data for family income of participants is presented in Table 3 (p. 38). Data profiles for the communities from which the children were drawn are portrayed in Table 4 (p. 39).

Table 1. Ethnicity of Sample.

Ethnicity	Frequency Experimental Group (n=41)	Percent	Frequency Control Group (n=30)	Percent
African-American	14	34	11	37
Hispanic	21	51	11	37
White	2	5	3	10
Native American	0	0	1	3
Asian	4	10	3	10
Other	0	0	1	3

Table 2. Ethnic Background of Sample by School.

School Site	Ethnicity	Frequency	Percent
School #1	African-American	3	21.4
N = 14	Hispanic	2	14.3
	White	2	14.3
	Asian	6	43
	Other	1	7
School #2	African-American	2	29
N = 7	Hispanic	4	57
	Asian	1	14
School #3	Hispanic	7	88
N = 8	White	1	12
School #4	African-American	4	31
N = 13	Hispanic	7	54
	White	2	15
School #5	African-American	16	55
N = 29	Hispanic	12	42
	Native American	1	3

Table 3. Family Income of Sample.

Family Income	Experimental (n = 41)		Control (n = 30)	
	n	%	n	%
Under $15,000	6	15	3	10
$16,000 - $25,000	7	17	2	7
$26,000 - $35,000	5	12	8	27
$36,000 - $45,000	7	17	6	20
$46,000 - $55,000	7	17	1	3
$56,000 - $65,000	1	2	5	17
Over $66,000	6	15	3	10

Table 4. Community Data Profiles.

Vital Condition	School #1	School #2	School #3	School #4	School #5
*Population	164,407	164,407	82,159	117,743	208,414
*Population <18	28,116	28,116	28,937	32,400	53,683
Children Receiving Public Assistance	33%	33%	60%	53%	59%
Teen Births	12%	12%	22%	19%	14%
Deaths due to AIDS	16%	16%	21%	20%	10%
Median Household Income	$20,325	$20,325	$10,628	$15,456	$22,175
Households Income <$10,000	29%	29%	50%	40%	27%
Children Below Poverty	30%	30%	43%	38%	40%
*Asian/Pacific Islanders	35.2%	35.2%	0.5%	2.7%	2.1%
*Blacks/African American	7.1%	7.1%	25.9%	35.7%	8.4%
*American Indian and Alaska Native	0.1%	0.1%	0.3%	0.2%	0.2%
*White Nonhispanic	28.2%	28.2%	1.3%	7.3%	13.6%
*Other Nonhispanic	0.4%	0.4%	0.2%	0.3%	0.3%
*Nonhispanic of Two or More Races	2.1%	2.1%	0.9%	1.7%	1.3%
*Hispanic	26.9%	26.9%	70.8%	52.1%	74.1%

Information taken from COMMUNITY DATA PROFILES, Administration for Children's Services (1998).

*Data was taken from the U.S. 2000 census

Program Sites

The mentoring programs took place in five urban Catholic schools that enrolled children from the local communities. An exception to this was School #2. This school is located in close proximity to two major companies and provides daycare before and after school hours. The school Principal reports that it draws many children of locally employed parents, who live in the suburbs. It is uncertain how many of these children from outside of the neighborhood participated in the study; however, School #2 students represent only 13% of the total sample.

All of the schools set aside a particular classroom, except one that provided a small lunchroom, in which the program took place. School administrators were highly supportive of the program. The locations offered privacy, adequate space and comfort.

Mentoring Program

The mentoring group format was developed and implemented by a local organization as a component of after-school programs. It accommodates 15 children per school, per year. The organization is a non-profit one that delivers coach/mentoring programs on life skills to children ages 7 to 12. The mission of the organization is to empower children to set and achieve goals, guide the children in pursuit of their goals, aid in developing personal responsibility, self-expression; and to acknowledge children for their effort and achievement. There is a set curriculum that addressed the following areas: self-awareness, team work, strengths, interests, values, understanding feelings and how to manage them, boundaries, decision making, goal setting and pursuing goals. There was a maximum of fifteen children per group and each group had two mentors.

Ten mentors were recruited and trained by the organization. All of them have earned at least a Bachelor degree, work in a professional environment and have had considerable experience working with children. They were given a detailed program description, with curriculum, and their role was explained to them. They signed a contract affirming their commitment for the fifteen weeks. All mentors had a lead coach and were given a coaching guide. They attended a full day of training, subsequent monthly training sessions and consulted by telephone with their lead coach weekly. They all received the same training and followed the same curriculum.

Operational Definition of Variables

The principal variables under investigation in this book are *mentoring*, the independent variable, and *self-efficacy*, the dependent variable. For the purposes of this research, *mentoring* is defined as the process in which a child receives the attention of an accomplished adult, serving as a role model during a peer group process. Group mentoring was the model used in this research project in an effort to increase the self-efficacy of children. A *mentor* in this research is defined as an accomplished adult who serves as a role model and group facilitator. The *mentor* provides opportunities to achieve individual goals, such as improving relationships with peers or siblings, or improving academic skills. The *mentor* assists the children through the process of goals, teaching life skills, and offering praise, support and encouragement. A child was considered mentored if he or she attended 13 out of 15 scheduled group mentoring sessions.

Self-efficacy is defined as the child's perception of his or her ability to carry out age-appropriate tasks, achieve goals, persevere and be proactive. This was measured by administering the Self-efficacy Scale Student Version to all child participants in the study and the corresponding Self-efficacy Scale Teacher Version completed by the teachers of each child participant (Fall & McLeod, 2001). The scales measured self-efficacy of the child based on performance.

Procedure

Prior to the onset of data collection, human subjects' review protocol were presented to the Human Subjects Committee of Adelphi University and approval was granted. The mentoring organization reviewed the research design, gave approval to proceed and assigned a liaison to oversee the project. The liaison had worked with the organization for three years and is an independent consultant who has conducted groups with urban school children for five years, coaching on life skills and goals.

Once approval was granted, the liaison and the author met with a representative from each school to explain the project and provide consent and demographic forms for distribution to parents. The Self-efficacy Scale Teacher Version was also presented to school representatives, with instructions for administering. Principals reported that teachers would be given time to complete the surveys during a weekly teacher meeting. The teachers were to be blind to the experimental condition of the children.

A monitor for the after-school programs was responsible for collecting data from the control group and their teachers. The author met with each monitor to explain the procedure. The liaison was in charge of coordinating timing of administering the questionnaires and collecting all forms from the schools. All schools were encouraged to contact the author by either phone or email with any questions pertaining to the project.

Each school provided a list of the children who met the criteria for participation. The larger schools selected a particular grade, as there were so many children in their after-school programs. An explanation of the project, consent forms and demographic information forms were sent home to the parents in a sealed envelope. Each envelope and the contents were assigned a code to ensure confidentiality. Information was returned, either by the child or the parent presented it to the after-school monitors when picking up the child. The envelopes remained sealed and were passed on to the author. Children who returned the consent forms were randomly assigned to either the mentoring program or wait-listed until the following year.

The program began in January 2004, following the winter break and each session was 90 minutes duration. The program ran for fifteen weeks. The first session of the program included introductions, getting acquainted, an explanation of what was included in the curriculum and completing the Self-efficacy Student Version pre-test. The mentors explained the items on the questionnaire and its purpose to the children. They were given a consent form to sign before it was administered. It was explained to the children that this was not a test, there were no right or wrong answers and their answers would remain anonymous. They were told that they may ask for help or clarification at any time. The subsequent group sessions included team work, strengths, interests and values, feelings, responding to feelings, setting boundaries, decision making, goal setting, goal projects, presentations and celebration. The children also took part in the regular after school curriculum, which included homework help, board games, arts and crafts, and in some schools music or dance. The control group participated in all of the other after-school activities with the exception of the mentoring program.

The Self-efficacy post-test and Children's Rating Scale for Bandura's Four Principal Sources of Self-efficacy (CRS) were administered by the author during the final session. It was again explained to the children that there were no right or wrong answers and they may ask questions at any time. Refreshments were provided and each child was given a small gift of a novelty pencil and pad of paper as a token of appreciation for their participation.

Instruments

Two versions of the Self-efficacy Scale were utilized for this research, the Self-efficacy Scale Student Version and the Self-efficacy Scale Teacher Version (Fall & McLeod, 2001). The scales were developed by Fall as an early screening tool to target school children deemed at risk for low self-efficacy and measure three principal effects of self-efficacy: choice behavior, persistence and attribution of failure. The scales were constructed to measure self-efficacy as perceived by the child and child self-efficacy as perceived by the teacher. Both scales have been determined as easy to complete in a short amount of time. Fall and McLeod make the assertion that children who score low on the teacher-rated scale may not exert much effort or persist at tasks and may attribute failure to causes outside of themselves. They assert that children, who score high, may believe that they have more choices, may exert more effort, persist at tasks and may attribute failure to lack of effort.

Self-efficacy Scale Student Version. This is a nine-item scale designed to reflect self-efficacious behaviors, as well as effects of self-efficacy. It is intended for children beyond second grade level. An example of a scale item measuring efficacious behavior is "When teachers give me new assignments or projects, I believe I can do them." An example of an item measuring an effect of self-efficacy is "It's easy to make choices." Answers reflect ratings from a four-choice Likert scale, with responses ranging from "Like me" to "Not at all like me." According to Fall and McLeod (2001), the scale yields a reliability coefficient, with Cronbach's coefficient alpha, of .64. A follow-up pre-test/post-test for student scale yielded a correlation of $r = .43$.

Self-efficacy Scale-Teacher Version. This is a nine-item scale with statements that correspond to the SES-SV. An example of a scale item demonstrating efficacious behavior in the child is "When presented with a new task, the child believes he or she can do it." An example of a scale item demonstrating the effects of self-efficacy in the child is "The child makes choices easily." A four-choice Likert scale is used for responses ranging from "Like the child" to "Not at all like the child". According to Fall and McLeod (2001), the scale yields a reliability coefficient, with Cronbach's coefficient alpha, of .94. Test-retest correlations were performed on the SES-TV for 53 students, with a 6-week interval between assessments to establish temporal stability. A significant correlation of r - .83, p < .001 was established. A follow-up pre-test/post-test for the teacher scale yielded a correlation of r = .83.

The studies conducted by Fall and McLeod (2001) demonstrate that the SES-TV appears to have greater reliability than the SES-SV. The SES-TV also showed evidence of factorial validity in accordance with Carmine and Zeller's 1979 guidelines.

Children's Rating Scale for Bandura's Four Principal Sources of Self-efficacy

This is a twelve-item instrument designed by the author to measure the extent to which the children in the experimental group perceived experiencing Bandura's four principal sources of self-efficacy during the course of their participation in the program. The four sources are mastery experience, vicarious experience, verbal persuasion and affective states. A sample question for *mastery experience* is "Since being in the group, I am able to do things that I did not do before."; for *vicarious experience* "I think if someone else my age can do it, so can I."; for *verbal persuasion* "My coaches encouraged me to keep trying".; and for *affective states* "When I understand my feelings, I do better". Each subscale consists of four items and is based on a Likert scale ranging from (4) "very much" to (1) "not at all". Reliability for this measure was computed using Cronbach's coefficient alpha. The results yielded a coefficient alpha of .78, with n of cases = 50, n of items = 12. This scale is presented on the following page.

Child Rating Scale for Bandura's Sources of Self-efficacy

1. The mentoring group offered me the opportunity to learn new skills.
   - ❏ Very much
   - ❏ A fair amount
   - ❏ Not too much
   - ❏ Not at all
2. Since being in the group, I am able to do things that I did not do before.
   - ❏ Very much
   - ❏ A fair amount
   - ❏ Not too much
   - ❏ Not at all
3. The group taught me how to achieve a goal.
   - ❏ Very much
   - ❏ A fair amount
   - ❏ Not too much
   - ❏ Not at all
4. I learned to do new things from watching the other kids.
   - ❏ Very much
   - ❏ A fair amount
   - ❏ Not too much
   - ❏ Not at all
5. I think if someone else my age can do it, so can I.
   - ❏ Very much
   - ❏ A fair amount
   - ❏ Not too much
   - ❏ Not at all
6. My group mentors taught me new skills.
   - ❏ Very much
   - ❏ A fair amount
   - ❏ Not too much
   - ❏ Not at all
7. My mentors said good things about me.
   - ❏ Very often
   - ❏ Fairly often
   - ❏ Not too often
   - ❏ Not at all
8. My mentors encouraged me to keep trying.
   - ❏ Very much
   - ❏ A fair amount
   - ❏ Not too much
   - ❏ Not at all
9. My mentors really believed in me.
   - ❏ Very much
   - ❏ A fair amount
   - ❏ Not too much
   - ❏ Not at all
10. My mentors helped me understand my feelings.
    - ❏ Very much
    - ❏ A fair amount
    - ❏ Not too much
    - ❏ Not at all
11. When I understand my feelings, I do better.
    - ❏ Very much
    - ❏ A fair amount
    - ❏ Not too much
    - ❏ Not at all
12. When I am not feeling good about myself, I don't want to try things.
    - ❏ Very much
    - ❏ A fair amount
    - ❏ Not too much
    - ❏ Not at all

Demographic Form. Parents were asked to complete a 15-item demographic information form. It was intended to gather the following information on the child: gender, age, grade, ethnicity, guardian (if not living with parent), number of siblings, birth order, number of siblings living in the home, and relationship to separated parents. It also collected the following information on the parent or guardian: level of education, marital status, employment, and gross family income.

Data Analysis

The author coded the data and entered the raw data in SPSS. Testing of the hypotheses was conducted with paired samples t-tests to determine whether there was a significant difference between the pre-test and post-test scores within groups and between groups, utilizing the SES-SV scores and SES-TV scores.

Pearson r correlations were used to compare the following:

1. Student and teacher pre-test for the experimental group.
2. Student and teacher pre-test for the control group.
3. Student and teacher post-test for the experimental group.
4. Student and teacher post-test for the control group.

T-tests were used to compare the following for significant differences:

1. Pre-test SES-SV scores to post-test SES-SV scores for experimental group.
2. Pre-test SES-SV scores to post-test SES-SV scores for control group.
3. Pre-test SES-TV scores to post-test SES-TV scores for experimental group.
4. Pre-test SES-TV scores to post-test SES-TV scores for control group.
5. Pre-test SES-TV scores for experimental group to pre-test SES-TV scores for control group.
6. Post-test SES-TV scores for experimental group to post-test SES-TV scores for control group.
7. Pre-test SES-SV scores for experimental group to pre-test SES-TV scores for control group.
8. Post-test SES-SV scores for experimental group to post-test SES-SV scores for control group.

The scores from the CRS measured whether the children experienced the sources of self-efficacy and to what degree. These scores were correlated with their self-efficacy scores. Pearson r Correlations were used to examine the relationship between answers on the questions from the CRS. Some of the data from demographic forms was used to determine the relationship between age, gender and self-efficacy and scores on the SES-SV and the CRS.

Limitations

There are several limitations that must be noted for this research investigation. The first is the external validity. Although the sample was random, it consisted of a convenience sample of Catholic school children participating in after-school programs. This minimizes the extent to which it can be generalized to other populations of elementary school children who attend public schools or do not have the added advantage of the activities provided by an after-school program. The second is the duration of the program. Fifteen weeks may not have allowed enough time for the children to receive the full benefits of the intervention. Learning new skills and using them takes time and practice. Third, some of the data was obtained from self-report measures. The children may have been biased in their answers and responded in a more favorable than accurate manner. This is further discussed in chapter six.

CHAPTER FIVE

Results

This chapter presents the findings of the research investigation presented in this book. First, the results of the hypotheses tests comparing the self-efficacy scores of two groups of children, those participating in a group-mentoring program with a group that was on a waiting list for the mentoring program are presented. Second, the results of the Children's Rating Scale will be presented. These findings determine if children perceived themselves as having experienced self-efficacy while participating in the group. Finally, some of the information from the demographic surveys will be presented as possible correlates of self-efficacy and as comparisons of the two groups.

Hypotheses

Hypothesis 1. Children participating in the mentoring program will demonstrate a significant increase in perceived self-efficacy scores from pre-test to post-test on the Self-efficacy Scale Student Version (SES-SV). Hypothesis 1 was examined using paired sample t-tests to compare the difference between pre-test and post-test means on the SES-SV for the experimental group. There was no significant difference between pre-test and post-test scores for the experimental group, $t = -1.223$, $df = 46$, $p = .228$. Thus Hypothesis 1 was rejected. (See Table 5)

Table 5. Paired Sample t-Tests for SES-SV Scores.

Self-efficacy Child Report								
Perceived Self-efficacy	**N**	**Pre-test M**	**SD**	**Post-test M**	**SD**	**t**	**df**	**p**
Experimental	47	28.48	4.21	29.40	4.81	-1.223	46	.228
Control	34	28.85	3.64	29.21	2.98	-.638	33	.528

Hypothesis 2. Children participating in the mentoring program will demonstrate significantly higher SES-SV scores at post-test than children in the control group. An Independent Samples t-test was used to test this hypothesis, comparing the post-test SES-

SV scores for the experimental group with those of the control group. The results yield no significant difference in scores, t = .169, df = 87, p = .866. Hypothesis 2 is therefore not confirmed. These results are shown in Table 6.

Table 6. Independent Group t-test Results for SES-SV Scores

Perceived Self-efficacy Child Report						
Group Pre-test	**N**	**M**	**SD**	**df**	**t**	**p**
Experimental	57	28.63	4.02			
				95	-.409	.683
Control	40	28.95	3.89			
Group Post-test				**df**	**t**	**p**
Experimental	50	29.40	4.67			
				87	.169	.866
Control	39	29.26	2.86			

Hypothesis 3. Children participating in the mentoring program will receive a significant increase in Self-efficacy Scale Teacher Version (SES-TV) scores from pre-test to post-test. *Hypotheses 3* was examined using paired sample t-tests to compare the difference between pre-test and post-test means on the SES-TV for the experimental group and the control group. The results indicate that the teachers reported a significant increase in self-efficacy for the children who participated in the mentoring program, $t = -4.099$, $df = 30$, $p = .000$. This confirms Hypothesis 3 as the children in the experimental group demonstrated a significant increase in SES-TV scores from pre-test to post-test. The findings for Hypotheses 3 are presented in Table 7 on the following page.

Table 7. Paired Sample t-Test for SES-TV Scores.

Self-efficacy Teacher Report								
Group	N	Pre-test M	SD	Post-test M	SD	t	df	p
Experimental	31	28.06	6.66	30.35	6.36	-4.099	30	.000**
Control	37	26.70	7.40	27.95	6.56	-1.517	36	.138

**p<.01

In summary, the paired sample t-test results confirm Hypothesis 3, which states that children participating in the experimental group would demonstrate significantly higher SES-TV scores from pre-test to post-test as reported by the teachers.

Hypothesis 4. Children participating in the mentoring program will demonstrate significantly higher SES-TV scores on the post-test than children in the control group. An Independent Samples t-test was used to test this hypothesis, comparing the post-test SES-TV for the experimental group with those of the control group. The results yield no significant difference in scores, $t = 1.528$, $df = 66$, $p = .131$. Hypothesis 4 is therefore not confirmed. These results are shown in Table 8.

Table 8. Independent Group t-Test Results for SES-TV Scores.

Self-efficacy Teacher Report						
Group Pre-test	N	M	SD	t	df	p
Experimental	34	28.20	6.52			
Control	46	26.08	7.25	1.347	78	.182
Group Post-test				t	df	p
Experimental	31	30.35	6.36			
Control	37	27.95	6.56	1.528	66	.131

Additional Analysis

Additional statistics were computed to analyze the Child Rating Scale (CRS) scores of the children who participated in the mentoring program. These scores rate the children's reported experience with Bandura's four sources of self-efficacy while participating in the mentoring program. This scale was created to determine if the children in the mentoring group actually perceived themselves as experiencing the sources of self-efficacy. As the scores indicate, children participating in the mentoring group perceived that they had experienced each of Bandura's (1997) four sources of self-efficacy, which included opportunities to learn new things and reach goals (performance accomplishments), vicarious learning, verbal persuasion and understanding physiological states. The results of these findings are displayed in Table 9.

Table 9. Percentages for Responses on the CRS.

Self-efficacy Sources and Corresponding Questions	Percentage of Responses N = 50			
	Not at all	Not too much	A fair amount	Very much
Mastery Experience				
1. Opportunities to learn	0%	2%	14%	84%
2. Able to do new things	4%	4%	18%	74%
3. Achieve goals	0%	4%	2%	94%
Average %	**1.3%**	**3.3%**	**11.3%**	**84%**
Vicarious Learning				
4. Learned from peers	20%	10%	32%	38%
5. Can do what peers do	2%	2%	20%	76%
6. Learned from mentors	0%	2%	16%	82%
Average %	**7.3%**	**5%**	**23%**	**65.3%**
Verbal Persuasion				
7. Mentor said good things	2%	4%	20%	74%
8. Mentor encouraged	0%	2%	14%	84%
9. Mentor believed in	0%	6%	6%	88%
Average %	**.7%**	**4%**	**13.3%**	**82%**
Feelings and Performance				
10. Understand feelings	0%	4%	12%	84%
11. Understand-do better	2%	4%	20%	74%
12. Not feeling good (reversed)	52%	18%	18%	12%
Average %	**18%**	**9%**	**17%**	**57%**

Pearson r Correlations were utilized to establish the strength of association between the twelve questions on the CRS. The findings indicate that the children perceived the mentors as having had a positive impact on their performance. There were significant correlations between the children's ability to "learn new skills", "be able to do things not able to do before", "achieve goals", "understand their feelings" and the group leaders "saying good things about them", "encouraging them to keep trying", "belief in them", and "helping them to understand how feelings affect performance". There were also correlations between "vicarious learning from peers" and "achieving goals". These findings suggest that the children were aware of the mentors' impact and that there is a relationship between the mentors' intervention and the children learning new things and achieving goals. The findings for these correlations are displayed in Table 10 on the following page.

Table 10. Pearson *r* Correlations for Child Rating Scale Items

	New Skills	New Things Learned	Goals	Vicarious Learning	Peer Ability	Coach Teach	Coach Say	Coach Encourage	Coach Belief	Understand Feelings	Feelings and Perform
New Things Learned	.408**										
Goals	.347*	.657**									
Vicarious Learning	.202	.202	.319*								
Peer Ability	.023	.146	-.040	.006							
Coach Teach	.640**	.312*	.325*	.111	.074						
Coach Say	.563**	.434**	.171	.217	.247	.384**					
Coach Encourage	.680**	.655**	.571**	.571**	.023	.537**	.563**				
Coach Belief	.480**	.341*	.291*	.169	-.044	.363**	.709**	.659**			
Understand Feelings	.584**	.449**	.297*	.210	.268	.639**	.602**	.584**	.489**		
Feelings and Perform	.492**	.228	.171	.108	.197	.384**	.293*	.208	.004	.539**	
Not Feel Good	-.124	.270	.022	.092	.319*	.000	.360*	.081	.032	.151	.105

N = 50   ** Correlation is significant at the .01 level.   *Correlation is significant at the .05 level

Correlations were utilized to compare student and teacher SES scores for the experimental and control groups. These results are displayed in Table 11.

Table 11. Pearson *r* Correlations for Pre-test and Post-test SES Total Scores.

	Exp. Child Pre SES Total	Exp. Child Post SES Total	Control Child Pre SES Total	Control Child Post SES Total
Experimental Teacher Pre SES Total	.584**			
Experimental Teacher Post SES Total		.170		
Control Teacher Pre SES Total			-.009	
Control Teacher Post SES Total				-1.33

**Correlation is significant at the 0.01 level

It was conjectured that some of the variables contained in the demographic form completed by the parents would have an impact on the SES-SV, SES-TV and CRS scores. Pearson r Correlations were performed to look at the relationship between age and the various scores on the instruments. The age of the child and Child Rating Scale for Bandura's Sources of Self-efficacy (CRS) scores were significantly negatively related ($r = -.449$, $p = .001$). There was a significant relationship between age and pre-test SES-SV scores for the control group ($r = .443$, $p = .001$). There was no significant relationship between age and SES-TV pre-test or post-test scores for the experimental or control groups. Gender was not related to scores. These findings are presented in Table 12 on the following page.

Table 12. Pearson *r* Correlations for Age, Gender, SES and CRS Scores.

Experimental Group	Age	Gender
Pre-teacher SES Scores	.048	.008
Post-teacher SES Scores	.058	.163
Pre-Child SES Scores	.176	.085
Post-Child SES Scores	-.214	-.092
CRS Scores	-.449**	-.204
Control Group		
Pre-teacher SES Scores	-.068	-.127
Post-teacher SES Scores	.238	-.081
Pre-Child SES Scores	.443**	.134
Post-Child SES Scores	.097	.012

**Correlation is significant at the 0.01 level

Summary of Findings

Hypothesis 1 was not confirmed, as there was no significant difference on the SES-SV from pre-test to post-test.

Hypothesis 2 was not confirmed, as the children in the experimental group did not demonstrate significantly higher scores on the SES-SV on post-test than the children in the control group.

Hypothesis 3 was confirmed, as the children participating in the mentoring program did demonstrate a significantly higher score from pre-test to post-test on the SES-TV than the children in the control group.

Hypothesis 4, was not confirmed as children participating in the mentoring program did not demonstrate a significantly higher score on the SES-TV post-test than the children in the control group.

The children participating in the mentoring group did report having experienced Bandura's four sources of self-efficacy while participating in the group, as indicated by their CRS scores. Several significant relationships among items on the CRS were found. There were positive relationships between learning new skills, being able to do new things, achieving goals and coach teaches, coach says, coach encourages. Coach believes in child, learning new skills, and being able to do new things was positively related to achieving goals. Learning new things was related to vicarious learning; and understanding feelings and the effect of feelings on performance was associated with learning new skills, coach says good things about child and coach teaches.

Looking at demographic variables: gender had no significant impact on SES-TV scores, SES-SV scores or CRS scores; there was a significant negative relationship between age and pre-test SES-SV scores for the control group; age had a significant influence on the responses to vicarious learning and peer ability on the CRS instrument and total CRS scores had a significant negative relationship to age.

CHAPTER SIX

Discussion

A discussion of this research investigation is presented in this chapter. Interpretations of the findings as they pertain to the variables of mentoring and self-efficacy are illustrated. Some of the discussion will focus on the sample of children who participated in the study and the benefits of group mentoring as a viable alternative to the traditional one to one mentoring. The chapter concludes with implications of the findings for social work education, theory and practice; and suggestions are offered for future research.

The Enhancement of Self-efficacy

The purpose of this research was to determine whether a group-mentoring program would increase the self-efficacy of child participants. Results show that this was indeed the case, according to teacher findings. Bandura asserts (1977) that when people experience the four sources of self-efficacy information, which are mastery experience, vicarious learning, verbal persuasion and interpretation of physiological states, self-efficacy is enhanced. What adds to the strength of the findings in the present study is that teachers were blind to which children participated in the mentoring program and children in both groups were nearly matched on all variables. However, children in the experimental and control groups rated themselves almost the same on the pre-test and the post-test scores for self-efficacy demonstrating no effect from the intervention according to their reports. This may be a reflection of the way children in this age group tend to rate themselves. This topic is discussed later in this chapter.

Bandura (1997) states that "efficacy builders" structure situations in which a person may achieve success by teaching the necessary skills, thus avoiding premature failure. He believes that opportunities for mastery experience offer the greatest enhancement of self-efficacy. This was taken into consideration and the four sources of self-efficacy information were introduced into the mentoring program utilized for this research project.

The emphasis was on achievement and the children were taught skills that would assist them with age-appropriate tasks and were offered opportunities to set and reach goals. It is not clear whether the mentors placed enough emphasis on feedback on achievement that would lead the children to believe that it was through their own capabilities that they achieved a goal. The author created an instrument to measure the children's experience of the four sources of self-efficacy, The Child Rating Scale for Bandura's Sources of Self-efficacy (CRS). Statistical findings for this scale indicate that the children responded favorably to all four sources, with *mastery experience* rated the highest with an 84% response to "very much". *Verbal persuasion* was the second highest rated source with 82% response to "very much". Yet the children in the mentoring program did not rate themselves any higher on self-efficacy post-tests than their peers in the control group.

The results of this investigation support the hypotheses that the children exposed to mentoring did demonstrate a significant increase in self-efficacy compared to similar children who did not receive mentoring, according to teacher report; and the CRS results indicate that the children who participated in the mentoring program strongly agreed that they experienced Bandura's four sources of self-efficacy. Further investigation is needed to devise methods to measure the children's experience more accurately.

Child Rating vs. Teacher Rating

The difference in child vs. teacher scores of child self-efficacy is an interesting dilemma to consider and Fall and McLeod (2001) explored this problem following a similar study in which they found that students rated themselves higher than teachers. They make the assertion that teachers are more reliable reporters and attribute this to their experience in evaluating and assessing students. It has also been suggested that children tend to rate themselves higher in an effort to appear socially acceptable. The children in Fall and McLeod's study were younger and they suggest that the age of the child may have had an influence on their interpretation of the questions. Another reason they provided for the differences between child and teacher scores was the reliability of the scale. They felt that the child rating scale was not as effective as the teacher rating scale.

It was used in the research presented in this book, as the author thought that the child rating scale still had merit. Contrary to the findings of Fall and McLeod (2001), there was no significant difference between teacher scores and children's scores on the self-efficacy pre-test; and children in the experimental group rated themselves nearly the same on the pre-test as teacher rated them. Thus, challenging the notion of Fall and McLeod (2001) that children tend to rate themselves higher than teacher ratings. Children in both groups also rated themselves nearly the same on post-test as pre-test. However, teachers' post-test ratings demonstrated that the children who received the mentoring had a significant increase in self-efficacy from the children who did not receive mentoring.

Some plausible explanations for the difference in children vs. teacher post-test scores in the research presented here may be that the children were not cognitively aware of their improvement. Additionally, the timing of the post-test may not have allowed the children to fully experience the effects of the mentoring group, or notice changes in their performance. In a review of the literature, it is noted, in several studies, that the post-test was given one day to a week following the intervention (Fall, 1999; Schunk, 1985; Schunk & Swartz, 1993). In the present research, it was given the last day of the program. It may be possible that the children need time to separate from the intervention and absorb its effects before assessing the impact. Although the research presented here did not fully support the idea of Fall and McLeod (2001), that children rate themselves higher than teachers, it is possible that their explanation that teachers are simply better raters of children's progress may hold true, to some extent, in the present research and explain the difference between the self-efficacy scores of mentored children and teachers. Schunk and Swartz have conducted extensive research with school children and make the statement that children have difficulty determining whether they are making progress in skills acquisition. It could be that children have difficulty, in general, assessing their own progress, but tend to judge themselves favorably as reported by Fall and McLeod (2001).

Self-efficacy and Self-regulated Learning

Although the purpose of the mentoring program was explained to the children initially, the research presented in this book may have contributed to the lack of increase in self-efficacy report by the children, as it did not emphasize the fact that the children were acquiring new skills and had the ability to use them, encouraging self-evaluation and self-regulatory learning. Had this been integrated into the program, the post-test scores of the experimental group may have yielded more favorable results.

Schunk (1995) states that self-evaluation must be linked with instruction and convey to the students that they are making progress. This is consistent with self-efficacy theory, which emphasizes that when children believe that success is a direct result of their effort, self-efficacy is enhanced (Bandura, 1997). While mentors in the program were educated on self-efficacy principals and how to introduce them into the program, they were not instructed to make the children cognizant of their presence and assess the impact on their performance. Perhaps the problem does not lie in the measure, but rather the method. Therefore, if we want to rely on the information provided by the children it is important to let them know that their efforts can make a difference in achievement, to explain the process more explicitly and to have them verbalize their progress. Perhaps the present research underestimated the importance of the children's evaluative reaction to their performance.

While the research presented here addresses some of the controversy over the accuracy of child self-rating, it is a rudimentary finding that necessitates the need for further research on this phenomenon to determine what factors intervene with children when rating their perception of self-efficacy.

Strength of Sample

Although the children were members of an after-school program, it is not a factor that would consider them different from a general population of children, as after-school programs, daycare and latch-key children have become a norm in our society (Fosarelli, 1992; Strober, 2004). What does differentiate them from the general population is the fact that they attend Catholic schools, which means that they go to a school with a faith-based orientation and receive religious education as part of their main curriculum. Another feature that distinguishes these students from the general population is that many of the parents or guardians pay tuition for the child's education. Some of the children attend on a scholarship or pay on a sliding-scale based on family income or number of siblings attending the school. Information for those children receiving scholarships or reduced tuition was not made available.

In a research report examining the academic performance of New York City Catholic elementary schools with city public schools, it was determined that Catholic school children surpassed their public school peers on New York State fourth and eighth grade test scores for mathematics and language arts (Domanico, 2001). The author further states that the results were apparent even with poor and minority children in the Catholic schools surpassing public school children in less poor districts. A similar study was conducted in Washington, D.C., using African-American Catholic and public school children and yielded similar conclusions, with Catholic school fourth and eighth grade students obtaining higher scores using the National Assessment of Educational Progress test results (Butler, 2000). No research data have been obtained to determine whether Catholic school children differ from public school children on self-efficacy or other related concepts such as self-esteem, self-concept or resilience.

It seems essential to discuss the relevance of applying the findings of the research presented in this book to the general population of children in the designated communities. The participants in the research presented here represented a convenience sample of Catholic school children that attended an after-school program. This raises the question: Do they differ significantly from their public school peers and if so, in what ways? A few reviews have been published on the differences between Catholic and public school children and mainly focus on academic achievement based on standardized scores (Butler, 2000; Domanico, 2001).

Domanico (2001) acknowledges that there are poor and minority students in the Catholic schools in New York City and yet the children surpass public school children on standardized math and English language arts test scores, regardless of race or family income. A feature that should affect scores is the teacher-student ratio, however, Catholic schools in New York City have a 1/ 21 student-teacher ratio while the public school ratio is 1/16.5 and yet the Catholic schools exceeded the public schools on test results. Similar results were obtained from a study performed by Butler (2000) in Washington D.C. area schools with fourth and eighth grade African-American students. A possible explanation for the success of Catholic schools on standardized tests may rest in Belfield's (2002) comments that religious schools tend to enroll less disabled students than public schools and they may also enroll fewer students with behavior problems. Belfield (2002) and Holland (1997) point out that the Catholic school ideology influences the children who attend, as families who identify with Catholicism and its ideals are apt to choose Catholic school for their children.

There may be other distinctions between Catholic school children and their public school peers. Holland (1997) states that there are five organizational characteristics that do distinguish Catholic schools from public schools that may contribute to their success in surpassing their public school counterparts on standardized tests. Catholic schools provide a core curriculum for all students, are embedded in a larger communal structure, are usually small enough to offer a sense of community, have decentralized governance and have an inspirational ideology reflecting organizational vision and values. It is possible that Catholic school ideology offers unique qualities that help children respond more favorably to intervention, but Holland (1997) makes the statement that many public schools also exemplify these characteristics.

The generalization of the research presented in this book hinges upon the compatibility between the Catholic school children and the public school children. While some Catholic school children mirror the ethnic background of the neighborhood, others differ. In this research project this is difficult to determine due to the small sample in some of the schools and the lack of individual school demographic data. School #1 is in a predominantly Asian neighborhood, which is reflected in the sample, with the majority (43%) of the children being Asian. This is higher than the community percentage of Asians in that district, which is 35.2%. Interestingly this school had 21.4 % African-American participants in the program and the Community Data Profile (New York City, 1998) only reflects 7.1% of African-Americans in the neighborhood. School #2 is in the same community district as School #1 but is the school that serves many suburbanites due to working parents placing their children in a school close to the workplace. This may explain the ethnic disparity between the children participating from this school and the community. Although the school is in a primarily Asian community, there were only 14% Asians who participated in this study and the major ethnic groups participating from School #2 are Hispanic (57%) and African-Americans (29%), although the community data shows 7% African-Americans and 27% Hispanics in the community. The community where school #3 is located is predominantly Hispanic (71%) and this is largely reflected in the research sample with 88% Hispanic. School #4 is also in a mainly Hispanic neighborhood (52%) and the sample represents this population with 54%

62

Hispanics. The African-American population in this community (36%) also closely matches the sample, which is 31%.

The community data representing income is not closely matched with the sample indicating that the neighborhoods are much poorer than what is reflected in our sample data. Based on data from the demographic profiles of participants, 13% of the families have incomes below $15,000. All of the schools had similar findings in this category except for school #1, which only had 7% of the families in the lowest income category. The community data information reports that, on average, 35% of household incomes in these community districts earn less than $10,000 per year. The poorest community being the one in which school #3 is located. The average income of these communities, as reported in the Community Data Profile (New York City, 1998), is $17,781.80 and the sample data indicate that the average income is 45% of the families earning between $15,000 – 35,000 per year. Thus it may be concluded that although many of the children may come from poor households and a large percentage living below the poverty level, this sample does not closely match the reported data for their communities on income.

Specific data for these Catholic schools was not available and it is quite possible that the complete data for the schools may mirror their communities more accurately. If this is not the situation and there is disparity between Catholic school children and public school children on income in these communities, it does not imply that the public school children do not have the capacity to increase their self-efficacy with intervention. Self-efficacy studies with children show that children from low-income families and other personal challenges do benefit from self-efficacy interventions (Brooks, 2006; Fall & McLeod, 2001; Fasko & Fasko, 1998; Harvey & Delfabbro, 2004; Jonson-Reid et al., 2005; Powers et al., 1995; Smokowski, 1998).

Fall (1999) indicated that poor children tend to have low self-efficacy scores but they were significantly raised with just six sessions of a play therapy intervention, as indicated by teacher reports. Jonson-Reid (2005) found that providing a support system that helped build African-American's belief in the importance of education helped raise academic self-efficacy. Powers and colleagues (1995) studied children with severe physical disabilities and the impact of mentoring by role models. The results indicated significantly higher levels of disability-related self-efficacy for those in the experimental group. This book, and the research presented therein, is based on the notion that all children have the potential to enhance their self-efficacy through intervention, apart from family income, ethnicity or personal challenges.

Group Mentoring vs. Individual Mentoring

A factor that distinguishes the research presented in this book from other studies employing mentoring is the group nature of the intervention. Most studies on mentoring involve a one mentor to one child model. The same mode is generally applied to self-efficacy interventions with one adult coaching a child during an individual task. Children yearn for peer interaction; want to be similar to peers and accepted by peers. They also need approval and validation from adult role models. Group mentoring offers a means of providing children with these essentials that contribute to healthy development. Research supports the effectiveness of group mentoring (Herrera et al., 2002; Saito & Blyth, 1992), as it provides the opportunity to interact with peers in the presence of supportive adults. These research investigations support the fact that mentoring improves social skills and communication and may lead to enhanced academic performance. While researching information for this book, there was no literature found to compare the effects of group mentoring with individual mentoring.

The present research did find that group mentoring enhanced the self-efficacy of the participants according to teacher report but found no significant difference in the child self-report. This issue was discussed above. Is it possible that children attributed the improved performance to the mentor or group experience, rather than seeing it as a direct result of their own effort? This raises another question – Would the children have perceived themselves as increasing their self-efficacy if they had had an individual mentor? The children may have thought that peers did well and learned new skills; therefore, they were able to improve their performance. However, Fall's (1999) study using one on one mentoring during play therapy sessions in an effort to enhance self-efficacy in young children had results consistent with this study.

The effects of group vs. individual mentoring remains a crucial question in this research investigation and one which only future research may answer. For future research, it would seem practical to compare the group model of mentoring with the traditional one to one mentoring, testing the same variables.

Limitations of the Child Rating Scale

The Child Rating Scale for Bandura's Sources of Self-efficacy was created for the research presented here to measure the children's perception of receiving mastery experience, vicarious learning, verbal persuasion and understanding physiological and affective states while participating in the mentoring group. The validity of the CRS may be questioned here as it was a new scale developed for this research and there was no test-retest reliability assessment taken. The children answered in a positive manner and there were many significant correlations among the items on the scale. It demonstrated that the mentors did have a positive impact on the children, who perceived themselves as having experienced all four of the sources of self-efficacy. This measure was presented to the children on the last day of the program, which was a day of celebration. It is possible that the anticipated festivities of the day contributed to the child's feelings of satisfaction toward the mentors. Waiting a day or up to a week before administering the CRS may have yielded different results.

Implications for Social Work Practice and Theory

Here the author explores the link between practice and theory and how self-efficacy theory operates within other theories that are applicable to social work practice. Social work practice has been based on theories drawn from other disciplines. Some of these theories are systems theory, cognitive theory, behavioral theory, empowerment theory and social learning theory. Theories allow us to conceptualize the problem and offer a method of approach. Although self-efficacy theory has psychological roots, it is consistent with longstanding social work tenets as it involves enhancing the extent to which one believes self to be capable, learning new skills, being proactive, achieving goals and acknowledges the importance of the person in environment. Bandura (1977) has identified self-efficacy as the missing link to understanding human behavior. He views human functioning as a dynamic interplay of personal, behavioral and environmental forces and states that self-efficacy beliefs are acquired through interactions with the environment. The information that influences self-efficacy beliefs is conveyed to us vicariously, persuasively, enactively and physiologically (Bandura). This involves cognitive and behavioral processes. The eminent approach to social work practice has been to view the problem in the context of the client's environment and we have learned how environment can shape clients' beliefs.

Lee (1996) talks about empowering theory that includes internal and external power. She describes external power as derived from social, political and economic influences and internal power as "releasing human potential" (p. 224). Self-efficacy can be seen as empowering clients as it helps clients recognize strengths and offers new ways of doing things. Bandura (1997) states that enhancing self-efficacy affects the choices we make and increases our ability to predict outcomes, exercising control over our environment, offering personal and social benefits. When clients feel efficacious and believe in their own capabilities, the environment is less threatening. Although they may not be able to change the environment, they will feel more competent to manage it. Self-efficacy theory is based on the belief in capability to achieve desired outcomes through human agency. People who feel capable think that their actions will achieve desired results.

Self-efficacy theory is consistent with social work values and theoretical perspectives and can be used in a variety of settings. Hepworth and Larsen (1990) speak of the value of self-efficacy in the social work profession and state that focusing on client strengths and alerting clients to the effect of their strengths in achieving goals may accomplish enhancing self-efficacy. They also mention how families and groups can serve as "resources" for promoting self-efficacy and discuss the crucial role that a social worker can make in "cultivating hope" and "...strengthen the clients' coping capacities and assist them to achieve their potentials ..." when the social worker has a sense of self-efficacy (p. 332).

The findings of this study indicate that intervention can be effective in enhancing self-efficacy beliefs in children, at least as perceived by their teachers. Although volunteer mentors were used in this study and not social workers, the author is a social worker and played a role in developing the curriculum and assuring that the principles of self-efficacy were carried out. Social workers already incorporate self-efficacy principles into their practice by providing feedback, acting as role models and building on the strengths of clients (Furstenberg & Rounds, 1995). Social workers can augment their clients' perceived self-efficacy by intentionally introducing the sources of self-efficacy as

66

in this group-mentoring model. Self-efficacy may be enhanced when social workers motivate and empower clients through their own strengths and offer them hope.

Strength-based models of practice emerged as an approach to working with the mentally ill in the early 1990's as an alternative to the pathology model (Saleebey, 1996). It has continued to develop as a form of intervention in social work and is used with various populations. The essence of strength-based practice is the belief that people have strengths and the ability to mobilize those strengths to make life better. People learn and gain strength from their environment. As social workers we can help clients discover and exercise their strengths. We are often the primary person who helps a client look at their circumstances through a different and more promising lens.

Studies of resilient children who seem to beat the odds regardless of their circumstances gave rise to research investigations to determine what distinguished these children from those who seemed vulnerable to their unfavorable life circumstances (Benard, 1991; Fraser et al., 1999; Garmezy, 1998; Howard & Dryden, 1999; Rutter, 1987). These investigators found that one of the most significant protective factors against unfavorable conditions was support of caring adults. These adults believed in the children, taught them different ways of looking at their situation but most of all helped give them the strength to overcome their circumstances. Although the children could not change their environments, they felt capable of managing it and made strides despite their position. In the present study, the teachers did see a difference in the children who participated in the mentoring program and children report on their CRS scores that the role of the mentor was the most influential component of their experience.

The guiding principles utilized in the mentoring program described in this study may be applied to social work practice with young people. The term *mentor* has been explicitly explored and defined in this study and encompasses a wide selection of adults in a child's life. A social work practitioner may take on the role of mentor for a child client by acting as a role model, providing positive verbal feedback, helping the child master goal achievement and understand the effect of physiological states on performance. In the present study, the implementation of self-efficacy was a social work intervention incorporated into the mentoring program. Social workers can advocate for

67

children and play a role in developing curriculum using self-efficacy principles for programs in schools and other places that work with young people.

Implications for Social Work Education

The findings of this study give encouragement to train social workers and social work students in techniques to deliberately utilize self-efficacy principles in practice. Recognizing children with low self-efficacy, based on their social and academic performance, offers a starting point for intervention. Self-efficacy theory can be used to help social work students conceptualize problems, develop plans of action in working with clients and provide tools for measuring outcomes by monitoring progress through mastering tasks and achieving goals. Self-efficacy theory is in keeping with basic social work practice as it looks at the unique interaction of person in environment, seeks to discover clients' strengths and encourage the use of those strengths. Applying the four principal sources of self-efficacy would involve helping clients set individual, realistic goals, acting as role models and providing feedback on progress toward reaching therapeutic goals and helping clients recognize and understand their physiological reactions. Through guidance of the social workers, clients would be encouraged to use their own talents and effort in learning new skills and making progress.

Although the research presented in this book has involved working with children, the same practices may be applied with adults and all clients experiencing challenges. Social work students can be taught to include these principles when working with clients. Teaching students to ask clients what their strengths are as well as their problems, partializing, breaking problems down into manageable components and helping clients use their own strengths to combat the problems and verbalizing those strengths can increase their self-efficacy. Self-efficacy of students may also be bolstered so that they in turn may enhance the efficacy of clients. When students believe something is possible and that they have the capability to achieve, it strengthens the intervention. This research has demonstrated that increasing knowledge and skills and providing positive feedback can enhance self-efficacy.

Suggestions for Future Research

The results of the research presented in this book indicate that self-efficacy can be enhanced in a group social setting with children. It provides a starting point for social work research on self-efficacy with children and is unique in that it used a group model of intervention. The research suggests that self-efficacy may be strengthened through the application of role models, vicarious learning, positive feedback, opportunities to achieve goals and understanding physiological states. The child participants rated their experience with the mentor's interactions and learning new things very highly. Future research could focus on the individual's components of self-efficacy to test the strength of each by dividing groups and applying different components to each group. As discussed above, the strength of the CRS is questionable. Although it provided useful information and reliability was established, further testing and re-testing is needed with this measure to assess its validity.

The present research focused on a group of children and took vicarious learning from peers into consideration. However, according to the CRS responses, children did not give as much credit to learning from peers as learning from mentors. This is in contradiction with Bandura's (1997) opinion that people learn best from models that are most like them. It appears that the adult role models in this study had a greater influence over the children than their own peers. Future research may focus on this development, looking at variables such as age and gender.

It is the belief of this author that an essential feature of any further research designed to determine the effect of interventions that enhance the self-efficacy of children should include promoting self-regulated learning. Verbal feedback by mentors, counselors, clinicians and encouraging the children to verbally express their progress can help achieve this. This allows the children to 'own' the experience and accomplishments.

Using Catholic school children compromised the generalization of this research. Future research should focus on various groups of children to draw out the variables that may contribute to successful enhancement of self-efficacy.

The present research utilized a very brief tool to measure self-efficacy. Introducing more items may help with accuracy of reporting. Another suggestion is using a second tool to measure the children's progress, such as the Connors Rating Scale or the Child Behavior Checklist. Applying qualitative methods of research could be beneficial and may yield more context-specific knowledge on the processes and outcomes of similar interventions.

Conclusion

Self-efficacy is a feeling of capability. It is an individual belief that one has what it takes to overcome obstacles and achieve desired outcomes. Acting as a social support, professionals working with children can apply the principles of self-efficacy theory to practice through serving as role models, providing verbal encouragement, positive feedback on progress, establishing opportunities for completing tasks, achieving goals and helping children understand how stress, from physiological states, affects performance.

The research presented in this book has demonstrated that directly applying the sources of self-efficacy with children can enhance their performance as recognized by teachers and that children report experiencing the sources of self-efficacy while participating in the mentoring program. Having an ongoing dialogue with children or clients regarding their strengths may further promote self-efficacy. Client empowerment is one of the foremost aims of social work. The process of empowering a client encompasses recognizing and mobilizing the client's strengths. Studies with young people have shown us that one person in the life of a child at risk for failure can make a difference (Benard, 1991; Frazer et al., 1999; Garmezy, 1998; Howard & Dryden, 1999; Rutter, 1987).

If introducing the sources of self-efficacy during a group-mentoring program with children can make a difference, this offers us a model of intervention to help raise the self-efficacy of children. As Bandura (1997) proclaims, self-efficacy beliefs help young people face challenges in an ever-changing society and can direct the course of a young person's life. It is the hope that the research presented here offers some guidelines to assist all those who work with children in helping them construct a more empowered and efficacious self, capable of confronting challenges and reaching their potential.

References

Alessandri, M. & Keating, L. (1995). Friends for youth: Program evaluation report San Jose, CA: Mentoring Institute.

Alter, C. F. (1996). Family support as an intervention with female long-term AFDC recipients. *Social Work Research, 20,* 203-216.

Bachay, J. B. & Cingel, P A. (1999). Restructuring resilience: Emerging voices. *Affilia, 14,* 162-175.

Bandura, A. (1977). *Social learning theory.* Englewood Cliffs, NJ: Prentice-Hall, Inc.

Bandura, A. (1995). *Self-efficacy in changing societies.* Cambridge UK: Cambridge University Press.

Bandura, A. (Ed.). (1997). *Self-efficacy: The exercise of control.* New York: W. H. Freeman and Company.

Bandura, A., Barbaranelli, C. Caprara, G. V., & Pastorelli, C. (1996). Multifaceted impact of self-efficacy beliefs on academic functioning. *Child Development, 67,* 1206-1222.

Bandura, A., Barbaranelli, C. Caprara, G. V., & Pastorelli, C. (2001). Self-efficacy beliefs as shapers of children's aspirations and career trajectories. *Child Development, 72,* 187-206.

Bandura, A. & Locke, E. (2003). Negative self-efficacy and goal effects revisited. *Journal Of Applied Psychology, 88,* 87-99.

Bandura, A. & Schunk, D. H. (1981). Cultivating competence, self-efficacy, and intrinsic interest through proximal self-motivation. *Journal of Personality and Social Psychology, 41,* 586-598.

Barron-McKeagney, T., Woody, J., & D'Souza, H. (2000). Mentoring at-risk Chicano Children and their parents: The role of community: Theory and practice. *Journal of Community Practice, 8,* 37-56.

Benard, B. (1993). Fostering resiliency in kids. *Educational Leadership, 51,* 44-50.

Bouffard-Bouchard, T. (1990). Influence of self-efficacy on performance in a cognitive task. *Journal of Social Psychology, 130,* 353-363.

Brendtro, L. K. & Longhurst, J. E. (2005). The resilient brain. *Reclaiming Children and Youth, 14,* 52-60.

71

Brooks, J. E. (2006). Strengthening resilience in children and youths: Maximizing
Opportunities through the schools. *Children & Schools, 28,* 69-75.

Brown, B. (1999). *Self-efficacy beliefs and career development* (Report No.EDO-CE-99-
205). Columbus, OH: Adult, Career, and Vocational Education. (ERIC Document
Reproduction Service No. ED429187).

Brown, W. K. (2004). Resiliency and the mentoring factor. *Reclaiming Children and
Youth, 13,* 75-79.

Butler, S. M. (2000). *Catholic schools.* Washington, D.C.: Momentum. (ERIC
Document Reproduction Service No. EJ603827).

Clement, S. (1987). The self-efficacy expectations and occupational preference of
females and males. *Journal of Occupational Psychology, 60,* 257-265.

Coleman, P.& Karraker, K.(2000). Parenting self-efficacy among mothers of school-age
children: Conceptualization, measurement and correlates. *Family Relations,
49,* 13-24.

Connell, J. P., Spencer, M. B., & Aber, J. L. (1994). Educational risk and resilience in
African-American youth: Context, self, action and outcomes in school. *Child
Development, 65,* 493-506.

Domanico, R. (2001). *Catholic schools in New York City.* New York: New York City
Board of Education. (ERIC Document Reproduction Service No. ED453309).

DuBois, D. L., Neville, A., Parra, G., & Pugh-Lilly, A. (2002). Testing a new model of
mentoring. *New Directions for Youth Development, 93,* 21-57.

Dubow, E. F., Arnet, M. Smith, K. & Ippolito, M. F. (2001). Predictors of future
expectations of inner-city children: A 9-month prospective study. *Journal of
Early Adolescence, 21,* 5-28.

Erdwins, C. (2001). The relationship of woman' role strain to social support, role
satisfaction, and self-efficacy. *Family Relations, 50,* 230-238.

Erin, R. M. (2006). The within person self-efficacy and performance relation. *Human
Performance, 19,* 67-87.

Fall, M. (1999). A play therapy intervention and its relationship to self-efficacy and
learning behaviors. *Professional School Counseling, 2,* 194-204.

Fall, M. & McLeod, E. H. (2001). Identifying and assisting children with low self-efficacy. *Professional School Counseling, 4*, 334-341.

Fasko, S. & Fasko Jr., D. (1998). A systems approach to self-efficacy and achievement in Rural schools. *Education, 119*, 292-300.

Fishman, R. & Stelk, W. (1997). The mentor school assistance program. *Preventing School Failure, 4*, 128-131.

Fosarelli, P. D. (1992). Latched alone. *NEA Today, 11*, 30-37.

Franzblau, S. H. & Moore, M. (2001). Socializing efficacy: A reconstruction of self-efficacy theory within the context of inequality. *Journal of Community and Applied Social Psychology, 11*, 83-96.

Fraser, M. W., Richman, J. M., & Galinsky, M. J. (1999). Risk, protection, and resilience: Toward A conceptual framework for social work practice. *Social Work Research, 23*, 131-143.

Furstenberg, A. & Rounds, K. A. (1995). Self-efficacy as a target for social work intervention. *Families in Society, 82*, 587-595.

Garmezy, N. (1983). Children in poverty: Resilience despite risk. *Psychiatry, 56*, 127-135.

Gilgun, J. F. (1996). Human development and adversity in ecological perspective, part 1: A conceptual framework. *Families in Society, 77*, 395-402.

Gillespie, D. & Hillman, S. (1993). *Impact of Self-efficacy Expectations on Adolescent Career Choices*. Paper presented at the Annual Meeting of the American Psychological Association, Toronto, Ontario.

Gilligan, R. (1999). Enhancing the resilience of children and young people in public care by mentoring their talents and interests. *Child and Family Social Work, 4*, 187-196.

Hackett, G. (1995). Self-efficacy in career choices and development. In A. Bandura (Ed.), *Self-efficacy in changing societies* (pp. 232-258). Cambridge UK: Cambridge University Press.

Hackett, G. & Betz, N. E. (1989). An exploration of the mathematics self-efficacy/ mathematics performance correspondence. *Journal for Research in Mathematics Education, 20*, 261-273.

Harvey, J. & Delfabbro, P. H. (2004). Psychological resilience in disadvantaged youth: A critical overview. *Australian Psychologist, 39*, 3-13.

Hepworth, D. H. and Larsen, J. (1990). *Direct social work practice, theory and skills* (3rd ed.). Belmont, CA: Wadsworth Publishing Company.

Herrera, C., Vang, Z., & Gale, L. (2002). *Group mentoring: A study of mentoring groups in three programs.* Philadelphia: Public/Private Ventures.

Holden, G., Barker, K. Meenaghan, T., & Rosenberg, G. (1999). Research self-efficacy: A new possibility for educational outcomes assessment. *Journal of Social Work Education, 35*, 463-479.

Holden, G. Meenaghan, T., Anastas, J., & Metrey, G. (2002). Outcomes of social work education: The case for social work self-efficacy. *Journal of Social Work Education, 38*, 115-133.

Holden, G., Wade, S., Mitchel, H., Ewart, C., & Islam, S. (1998). Caretaker expectations and the management of pediatric asthma in the inner city: A scale development study. *Social Work Research, 22*, 51-58.

Holland, P. B (1997). *Catholic school lessons for the public schools.* School Administrator. (ERIC Document Service Reproductions No. EJ548964)

Horn, L. J., Chen, X. (1998). *Toward Resiliency: At-risk Students Who Make It to College.* Washington, D. C.: U. S. Department of Education, Office of Educational Research and Improvement.

Howard, S. & Dryden, J. (1999). Childhood resilience: Review and critique of Literature. *Oxford Review of Education, 25*, 307-323.

Jackson, A. P. (2000). Maternal self-efficacy and children's influence on stress and Parenting among single black mothers in poverty. *Journal of Family Issues, 21*, 3-16.

Jackson, A. P. & Huang, C. H. (1998). Concerns about children's development: Implications for single employed black mothers' well being. *Social Work Research, 22*, 233-240.

Jonson-Reid, M., Davis, L., Saunders, J., Williams, T., & Williams, J. H. (2005). Academic self-efficacy among African American youths: Implications for social work practice. *Children & Schools, 27*, 5-14.

Katz, M. (1997). Overcoming childhood adversities: Lessons learned from those who have "beat the odds". *Intervention in School & Clinic, 32*, 205-210.

Keating, L. M., Tomishima, M., Foster, S., Alessandri, M. (2002). The effects of a mentoring program on at-risk youth. *Adolescence, 37*, 717-734.

Kim-Cohen, J., Moffitt, T. E., Caspi, A., & Taylor, A. (2004). Genetic and environmental processes in young children's resilience and vulnerability to socioeconomic deprivation. *Child Development, 75*, 651-658.

Kwok, S. & Wong, D. (2000). Mental health of parents with young children in Hong Kong: The roles of parenting stress and parenting self-efficacy. *Child and Family Social Work, 5*, 57-65.

Lee, J. (1999). The positive effects of mentoring economically disadvantaged students. *Professional School Counseling, 2*, 172-178.

Lee, J. (1996). The empowerment approach to social work practice. In F. J. Turner (Ed.), *Social Work Treatment* (pp. 218-249). New York: The Free Press.

Linnenbrink, E. A. & Pintrich, P. (2003). The role of self-efficacy beliefs in student engagement and learning in the classroom. *Reading & Writing Quarterly, 19*, 119-137.

Little, M. , Axford, N., & Morpeth, L. (2004). Research review: Risk and protection in the context of services for children in need. *Child and Family Social Work, 9,* 105-117.

Markus, H. & Nurius, P. (1986). Possible selves. *American Psychologist, 41*, 954-968.

McCluskey, K. W., Noller, R., Lamoureux, K., & McCluskey, A. (2004). Unlocking hidden potential through mentoring. *Reclaiming Children and Youth,13*, 85-93.

Melamid, E., Nemetsky, J., Simpson, L., & Ziegler-Madden, J. (1998). Community data profiles. *New York City Administration for Children's Services.*

McMillan, J. H. & Reed, D. (1994). At-risk students and resiliency: Factors contributing to academic success. *Clearing House, 67*, 137-142.

Mitchell, H. J. (1999). Group mentoring: does it work? *Mentoring & Tutoring, 7*, 113-120.

Montcalm, D. M. (1999). Applying Bandura's theory of self-efficacy to the teaching of research. *Journal of Teaching in Social Work, 19*, 93-105.

75

O'Donnell, J., Michalak, E., & Ames, E., (1997). Inner-city youths helping children: After-school programs to promote bonding and reduce risk. *Social Work in Education, 19*, 231-241.

Pajares, F. & Miller, M. (1994). Role of self-efficacy and self-concept beliefs in mathematical problem solving: A path analysis. *Journal of Educational Psychology, 86*, 193-204.

Palmer, N. (1997). Resilience in adult children of alcoholics: A nonpathological approach to social work practice. *Health & Social Work, 22*, 201-09.

Parra, G. R., DuBois, D., Neville, H., & Pugh-Lilly, A. (2002). Mentoring relationships for youth: Investigation of a process-oriented model. *Journal of Community Psychology, 30*, 367-388.

Patrick, H. & Hicks, L., & Ryan, A. M. (1997). Relations of perceived social efficacy and social goal pursuit to self-efficacy for academic work. *Journal of Early Adolescence ,17*, 109-128.

Pintrich, P. R. & De Groot, E. V. (1990). Motivational and self-regulated learning components of classroom academic performance. *Journal of Educational Psychology, 82*, 33-40.

Powers, L. E., Sowers, J., & Stevens, T. (1995). An exploratory, randomized study of the impact of mentoring on the self-efficacy and community-based knowledge of adolescents with severe physical challenges. *Journal of Rehabilitation*, 33-41.

Rak, C. F. & Patterson, L. E. (1996). Promoting resilience in at-risk children. *Journal of Counseling & Development, 74*, 368-373.

Rhodes, J. E. (1994). Older and wiser: Mentoring relationships in childhood and adolescence. *The Journal of Primary Prevention, 14*, 187-196.

Rhodes, J. E., Grossman, J. B., & Roffman, J. (2002). The rhetoric and reality of youth mentoring. *New Directions for Youth Development*. 93, 9-20.

Rosenfeld, L. Richman, J., & Bowen, G. (2000). Social support networks and school outcomes: The centrality of the teacher. *Child and Adolescent Social Work Journal, 17*, 205-226.

Rutter, M. (1987) Psychosocial resilience and protective mechanisms. *American Journal of Orthopsychiatry, 57*, 316-331.

Saito, R. N. & Blyth, D. (1992). *Understanding mentoring relationships*. Minneapolis, MN: Minneapolis Youth Trust.

Saleebey, D. (1996). The strengths perspective in social work practice: Extensions and cautions. *Social Work, 41*, 296-305.

Scheel, M. J. & Rieckmann, T. (1998). An empirically derived description of self-efficacy and empowerment for parents of children. *American Journal of Family Therapy, 26*, 15-27.

Schofield, G. & Brown, K. (1999). Being there: a family center worker's role as a secure base for adolescent girls in crisis. *Child and Family Social Work, 4*, 21-31.

Schunk, D. H. (1983). Enhancing self-efficacy and achievement through rewards and goals: Motivational and informational effects. *Journal of Educational Research, 78*, 29-34.

Schunk, D. H. (1985). Participation in goal setting: Effects on self-efficacy and skills of learning-disabled children. *The Journal of Special Education, 19*, 307-317.

Schunk, D. H. (1990). Goal setting and self-efficacy during self-regulated learning. *Educational Psychologist, 25*, 71-86.

Schunk, D. H. (1995). *Learning goals and self-evaluation: Effects on children's cognitive skills acquisition*. Paper presented at the Annual Meeting and Exhibit of the American Educational Research Association, San Francisco, CA.

Schunk, D. H. (1996). *Self-efficacy for learning and performance*. Paper presented at the Annual Conference of the American Educational Research Association, New York, NY.

Schunk, D. H. & Gunn (1986). Self-efficacy and skill development: Influence of task Strategies and attributions. *Journal of Educational Research, 79*, 238-274.

Schunk, D. H. & Swartz, C. W. (1993). Writing strategy instruction with gifted students: Effects of goals and feedback on self-efficacy. *Roeper Review, 15*, 225-230.

Schunk, D. H. & Zimmerman, B. (1997). Social origins of self-regulatory competence. *Educational Psychologist, 32*, 195-208.

Shih, S. & Alexander, J. M. (2000). The interacting effects of goal setting and self- or other-referenced feedback on children's development of self-efficacy and cognitive skill within the Taiwanese classroom. *Journal of Educational*

Psychology, 92, 536-543.

Smokowski, P. R. (1998). Prevention and intervention strategies for promoting resilience in disadvantaged children. *Social Service Review, 98*, 337-364.

Strober, M. H. (2004). Children as a public good. *Dissent, 51*, 57-61.

Terry, J. (1999). A community/school mentoring program for elementary students. *Professional School Counseling, 2*, 237-240.

Townsel, K. T. (1997). Mentoring African American youth. *Preventing School Failure, 43*, 125-129.

Turner, F. J. (Ed.). (1996). *Social Work Treatment.* (4th ed.). New York: The Free Press.

Weinberg, D. H. (1999). *Press Briefing on 1998 Income and Poverty Estimates.* Washington D.C.: U. S. Census Bureau.

Werner, E. E. (1995). Resilience in development. *Current Directions in Psychological Science, 4*, 81-85.

Werner, E. E. & Smith, R. S. (1992). *Overcoming the odds: high risk children from birth to adulthood.* Ithaca, NY: Cornell University Press.

White, K., Hohn, R. L. & Tollefson, N. (1997). Encouraging elementary students to set realistic goals. *Journal of Research in Childhood Education, 12*, 48-57.

Winfield, L. F. (1991). Resilience, schooling and development in African-American Youth. *Education & Urban Society, 24*, 5-14.

Zimmerman, B. J. (1995). Self-efficacy and educational development. In A. Bandura (Ed.), *Self-Efficacy in Changing Societies* (pp. 202-231). Cambridge UK: Cambridge University Press.

Zimmerman, B. J. & Martinez-Pons, M. (1990). Student differences in self-regulatory learning: Relating grade, sex and giftedness to self-efficacy and strategy use. *Journal of Educational Psychology, 182*, 51-59.